The
CIGAR LOVER'S
COMPENDIUM

The CIGAR LOVER'S COMPENDIUM

EVERYTHING YOU NEED TO LIGHT UP AND LEAVE ME ALONE

LAWRENCE DORFMAN

LYONS PRESS
Guilford, Connecticut
An imprint of Globe Pequot Press

Given the constantly changing legalities that surround smoking, some of the
stores listed in the back of this book may no longer be in business.

To buy books in quantity for corporate use
or incentives, call **(800) 962-0973**
or e-mail **premiums@GlobePequot.com.**

Lyons Press is an imprint of Globe Pequot Press.

Text design by Sheryl P. Kober
Text layout by Melissa Evarts

Library of Congress Cataloging-in-Publication Data

Dorfman, Lawrence.
 Cigar lover's compendium : everything you need to light up
and leave me alone / Lawrence Dorfman.
   p. cm.
 ISBN 978-1-59921-937-0
 1. Cigars. 2. Cigar smoking. I. Title.
 TS2260.D67 2010
 679'.72—dc22

                                       2010022248

Printed in the United States of America

10 9 8 7 6 5 4 3 2 1

To A Segar

Sweet antidote to sorrow, toil, and strife,
Charm against discontent and wrinkled care.
Who knows thy power can never know despair;
Who knows thee not, one solace lacks of life:
When cares oppress, or when the busy day
Gives place to tranquil eve, a single puff
Can drive even want and lassitude away,
And give a mourner happiness enough.
From thee when curling clouds of incense rise,
They hide each evil that in prospect lies;
But when in evanescence fades thy smoke,
Ah! what, dear sedative, my cares shall smother?
If thou evaporate, the charm is broke,
Till I, departing taper, light another.

—Samuel Low (circa 1801)

O METAPHYSICAL TOBACCO
O metaphysical Tobacco,
Fetched as far as from Morocco,
Thy searching fume
Exhales the rheum,
O metaphysical Tobacco.

—MICHAEL EAST (1606)

CONTENTS

Groucho Marx

FOREWORD

*M*ore than a decade has passed since the cigar boom of the 1990s. The hype over Cuban cigars is gradually fading. Do not misinterpret me, there are still some good Cuban cigars out there, but the prime quality tobacco once available in Cuba in years past, as well as the cigar construction standards in that country, have declined noticeably. Now, another boom of sorts is taking place in the cigar industry. As an avid smoker, connoisseur, collector, and specialist of fine cigars, I cannot neglect the outstanding quality of taste and construction of cigars now available from around the world. Some of the top producers of the new boom include Don Pepin Garcia, Oliva Cigars, Illusione, Perdomo, Padron, Tatuaje, and other large producers that make fine cigars with tobacco from other geographical areas. Punch, a Honduran brand, recently released a Nicaraguan-grown tobacco cigar. J. C. Newman, Ashton, Davidoff, and Felipe Gregorio also consistently release new cigars using fine tobacco from many different regions.

Just like fine wine, tobacco inherits its flavor from climate, soil, and growing conditions. The Nicaraguan volcanic soil and climate are very similar to that of Cuba. Many of the newer Nicaraguan, Honduran, and Dominican brands are comparable to the great Cuban cigars of years past.

There has been much discussion concerning health issues related to cigar smoking. I have read many articles on the risks that include misinformation provided by the big pharmaceutical companies on the dangers of smoking cigars.

There have also been many studies that are not as well known that refer to the benefits of smoking cigars. The FDA recently got the power to regulate the tobacco industry. The real truth is that, like most things we indulge in for pleasure, cigar smoking may be harmful if not done in moderation. No studies conclude that smoking one or two cigars a day can be harmful to your health. On the contrary, many stories from fellow cigar smokers relate how cigars benefit their mental health.

Cigar smoking is relaxing and helps banish anxieties. For me, taking time out of a stressful day to enjoy a cigar is calming and helps relieve that stress.

When I travel I always find cigars. I have been to many cigar events and seminars and have made love of cigars my career and livelihood. One of my favorite places in the world to experience the history and lifestyle of the cigar is Ybor City in Tampa, Florida. In the early 1900s, Ybor City was the cigar capital of the world. Ybor was home to many cigar factories that produced most of the cigars smoked in the United States during this time. Today the historic preservation of 7th Avenue and the surrounding city takes you back to that time. In the many cigar shops and lounges in Ybor City, cigars are made right on the premises. No cigar lover would want to miss the Cigar Heritage Festival held each November in the center of Ybor City. Many other events take place all over the country each year, and I recommend you attend one if the opportunity arises.

In my early days, I found a tremendous camaraderie among cigar smoking guys and gals. Yes, many women enjoy sitting back and enjoying a cigar. I have visited hundreds of cigar shops across the world, and the people I meet are there to enjoy the fellowship of other smokers and their common interest in cigars.

One quality that I have experienced among smoking comrades is that, in many cases, the sharing and offering of cigars is a common occurrence. I find it a pleasure to share my knowledge and to offer cigars that I enjoy to someone who may not have tried a particular brand. The shared experience means a lot to the people I have met.

So sit back, light up, and savor the cigar. And the experience.

—Bill Raffaele, Cigar Manager
The Owl Shop, New Haven, Connecticut

ACKNOWLEDGMENTS

I want to thank RP for loving the smell of a great cigar and for encouraging me to smoke wherever and whenever I want.

The Owl Shop—a life-saving smoker's oasis in a sea of smoke Nazis.

Glen, Joe, Bill, and the gang—making the art of smoking a true joy.

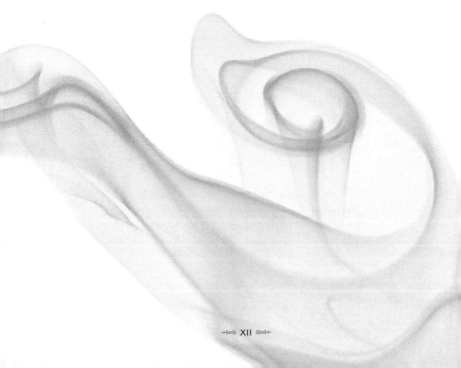

INTRODUCTION

"Sometimes a cigar is just a cigar."

—SIGMUND FREUD

Cigar: A tightly rolled bundle of dried and fermented tobacco, which is ignited so that its smoke may be drawn into the smoker's mouth.

Cigar: A cylindrical roll of cured tobacco leaves for smoking, perhaps from Mayan *sicar*, meaning, "to smoke."

Cigar: From the Spanish *cigarro* (cigar), which was perhaps derived from the Spanish *cigarra* (cicada).

There's always been a lot of confusion surrounding the first cigars. Where did they come from? Who invented them? Was it Christopher Columbus or was it the Cubans? Or was it someone long before that? Well, I can tell you this much: Cigars have been around for a long while. There is even some evidence that the use of tobacco in this form can be traced back to the tenth century, as can be seen in the decorations on primitive urns that depict the figures of men smoking cigars.

And one could safely bet that these figures of men were outside of their homes and hiding from their wives.

Yes, the cigar life has often been a difficult one. While most men love 'em—and many women too—there are those who hate 'em with the heat of a supernova and go crazy when someone lights one up in their presence. You've all seen the face . . . you know, the one that looks like someone put an old piece of onion that's been covered in garlic and sardines and left out in the garbage for three weeks in the trashcan during the middle of the summer under the person's nose. Am I right? Well, I'm here to tell you: Screw those people.

Cigars are a wonderful thing and history proves it out. Having a cigar has always been the best way to stop, relax in the moment, and take stock. They've been used to celebrate the birth of a child or a new job, to point up a great wine or a special after-dinner drink . . . but mostly, they have come to signify a camaraderie, a bond that brings people together under a shared vice.

This book is a collection of stuff about cigars. Sure, there's the prerequisite information about the history, about how to choose the best stick, about what the sizes are and what the ring gauges mean . . . all good stuff, to be sure. You'll learn to talk the talk.

But what is this thing, *compendium*? The meaning in the dictionary is "A short, complete summary; an abstract or a list or collection of various items." Basically, stuff you wanna know.

It's all that and a bag of chips—a complete collection for your reading enjoyment.

Let's start at the beginning.

Tell me, Mr. Cigar Guy, why smoke cigars?

It's a good question. They make your clothes smell, your breath stink, and, as mentioned before, can incur the wrath of many. There are those who say the mere *act* of smoking a cigar in these smoke Nazi–infested times is one so vile that there is very little to rival it. They would point to killing baby seals as a comparable evil deed . . . or, at the very least, making those cute little guys smoke cigars.

And it doesn't stop there. It's not enough that these folks consider cigar-smoking to be a disgusting habit. Oh, no . . . throughout the years, there has even been copious ridiculous legislation enacted to diminish it, slow it down, or stop it.

The arcane and often random laws that have sprung up in the past years are mind-boggling. A small sampling:

New Orleans, Louisiana: A city known for guilty pleasures, New Orleans possesses a law that prohibits anyone participating in a carnival or parade from using tobacco products while doing so. In addition to this, a No Smoking sign must be visibly attached to all parade floats.

Not that any of the mostly male onlookers, with hundreds of nubile bare-chested ladies throwing beads, are really paying attention.

New Jersey: While a sign reading Do Not Feed the Animals is common in many zoos, New Jersey takes this notion one step further with a law that prohibits people from giving cigars or whiskey to local zoo animals.

Cigarettes and beer are fine, though. But be careful, it may lead to evolution.

South Bend, Indiana: It is illegal to make a monkey smoke a cigarette. This law goes back to 1924 when a monkey was found guilty of the crime of smoking a cigarette and forced to pay a fine of $25, as well as trial costs.

There is no information available as to whether the monkey was able to come up with the money.

Newport, Rhode Island: A law prohibits people from smoking a pipe after sunset.

You know, when the sun goes down, all manner of craziness can occur—vampires, werewolves, and argyle sweaters.

Marceline, Missouri: Minors are allowed to purchase rolling papers and tobacco but aren't allowed to purchase lighters.

Hmm . . . how am I going to light this? If only there was some way to make fire. . . . Hey, I know! Matches!

You get the picture.

So how does the average cigar smoker fight this terrible persecution? By smoking as many cigars as you can, as often as possible.

But first things first. To answer the primary question posed—why smoke cigars?

The answer is not so simple, grasshopper. The answer is . . . wait for it . . . you have to try it to know. The answer is in the doing. I know, I know . . . that's not really an answer. Perhaps a tad too Zen?

Well, okay, I'll try to give you a more tangible response. One, smoking cigars has tradition attached to it. Cigars have been used to close or seal a deal, to celebrate a life event, or to just take a long pause (or pauses) and reflect, relax, kick back, enjoy your life, enjoy your friends, and be in the moment.

(Again with the Zen?)

Okay, how about . . . because once the bug bites, once you've had a top-quality, well-made cigar, you will begin to understand. You will realize that the benefits are myriad—that the taste is spectacular, that the calming effect equals those of Percocet and Darvon, that the camaraderie surrounding the cigar smoker is unparalleled . . . and that you can look very cool doing it.

And you will be joining a club that would indeed have you as a member (my sincerest apologies to Groucho).

Some of the greatest minds and greatest personalities in the history of the world smoked cigars: Winston Churchill was supposed to have smoked *at least* eight to ten cigars a day and is still associated closely with cigars to this day. You can't think about him or George Burns or Sigmund Freud or Ernest Hemingway without visualizing a stogie strategically placed between his lips. Red Auerbach, Orson Welles, Al Capone . . . the list goes on forever. The great and the near-great all smoked cigars, and countless others as well.

Viscerally, the cigar can do a bunch of things. Besides pointing up the taste of great booze, fine wine, or even beer . . . besides making a sporting event all that much more fun to witness, live or on a screen . . . besides making boating and fishing and a host of endeavors that much more fun . . . they just taste great.

Ultimately, the point of this book is to have, in the palm of your hand, a fun, irreverent little reference guide. Can it be used as ammunition against the naysayers? Definitely. Will it be a minor cigar education on every page? Indubitably. Is it something to start up the conversation at the bar? You betcha. But ultimately, it's just a lot of fun.

Take it on the road. Take it to a party. Take it to your favorite cigar bar. Or take it to the beach and read it as you light up. But, by all means, have fun reading it and smoke 'em if you got 'em. It'll be worth the effort.

Enjoy.

Chapter 1

A LITTLE CIGAR HISTORY

HISTORY ON THE PAGE CAN BE A LITTLE DRY. AND DRY ISN'T A GOOD thing when talking about cigars. But the European discovery of tobacco and the introduction of cigars to a cigar-hungry continent (even though they didn't know it yet) should be noted as a major happening when discussing any cultural events in the world's history.

In 1492, when Columbus sailed the ocean blue to the Americas, he dispatched two of his sailors to an island 90 miles from the mainland, an island that would eventually become known as Cuba. There, the sailors witnessed the smoking and inhaling of burned leaves through a pipe, a medicinal and religious rite that looked curiously appealing. The sailors were fascinated by the natives' puffing (it can do that to you) and brought *tobacco* (which was actually the native name for the pipe) and *cohiba* (the leaves) back to Europe with them.

It took almost a century for tobacco (the Europeans applied that name to the leaves) to make the transition from medicine to luxurious habit to, finally, fashion. But make its way it did and the practice of smoking soon spread throughout Europe, and then all the way east to China.

Arguably, Cuba is the birthplace of the cigar. In the sixteenth century, it was the first region in the New World to understand and

Winston Churchill

take advantage of the impending European demand for tobacco. In the eighteenth century, Cuba's innovation of the cigar virtually cemented its lead in tobacco exporting.

However, the cigar didn't even get close to the marvelous product of tobacco engineering we know today until the beginning of the eighteenth century, when the concept of the rolled tube (which had been pioneered in Cuba) eventually made it's way to Seville. From then on, cigars were all the rage in Spain and Portugal. Soldiers from England, France, and Germany, fighting in various wars, quickly adopted the practice of smoking the cigars after they'd purloined them from the Spanish, spreading the habit to their friends and family back home.

Back in the States, in 1762, a British Army colonel, Israel Putnam, introduced to the colonies cigars that he had brought back from Cuba. A native of Connecticut, Putnam's influence would later have a huge impact on the use of Connecticut leaf in the making of cigars. (Connecticut, for reasons still unknown to this day, has a weird combination of soil and climate and a mystical "something else," which has made for the industry's best wrappers).

As the colonies still tended to emulate the Brits and the "continent," cigar smoking started to flourish in the more refined societal circles. They were also quite expensive so cigars became the *de rigueur* pastime for the elite and wealthy.

The increased demand was taking its toll in tobacco country. Back in Cuba, tobacco exporters were encountering a bit of a rough period. As the large factories began to push out the small, peasant-owned farming lots, there began a consolidation of tobacco production, with the number of factories dropping from over one thousand to just over one hundred in a period of about fifty years. Following this consolidation, the mid 1800s saw the birth of the more sophisticated brands and style differentiation—a development that directly fathered many of the major brands and cigar styles known throughout the world today.

The end of the nineteenth century also ended Cuba's patience with Spanish oppression. Thanks to the Spanish-American War, Spain was now out of the picture while the island began to enjoy much greater influence from its nearby neighbor, the United States, which was hungry for what Cuba produced, especially tobacco. This relationship further fueled cigar exports to North America—that is until the overthrow of Cuban dictator Fulgencio Batista in 1959 by Fidel Castro and his rebels, which set off a smaller version of the Cold War that continues to this day. The United States didn't trust Castro and Castro didn't trust the United States, and all this mistrust led to an American embargo against Cuba in 1961—of which cigars were a major part. This led Cuba to spend the last half of the twentieth century fighting the threat of American machine-made cigars and the loss of revenue from the largesse it lost after the fall of the Soviet Union.

Cigar smoking in the United States didn't really see a boom until around the time of the Civil War, with well-recognized individual brands not emerging until the end of the nineteenth century. By then the cigar had become an American status symbol. By that time, cigar smoking had become so popular among gentlemen in Britain and France that European trains introduced smoking cars to accommodate them, and hotels and clubs boasted smoking rooms. The after-dinner cigar, accompanied by a glass of port or brandy, became an honored tradition and a mark of refinement. This ritual was given an added boost by the fact that the Prince of Wales, the future Edward VII and a fashion trendsetter, was a cigar devotee, much to the annoyance of his mother, Queen Victoria, who disliked any kind of smoking. (The low-end King Edward cigar was likely named in his honor, though he probably would have turned his nose up at them.)

The popularity of cigars dramatically ebbed and flowed in the 1960s and '70s. However, starting in the late '80s, there was a major revival in the popularity of handmade cigars, which continues to this day. Cigars have become chic again, thanks to the enthusiasm shown for them by celebrities, politicos, and sports stars. Not even Bill Clinton's famous cigar escapade with Monica Lewinsky dampened the public's enthusiasm for good cigars. The hardcore smokers have always stayed true to the pastime.

Based on a number of surveys, the cigar smoking population in the United States is estimated to be somewhere between four and five million people.

Worldwide, the United States is the top consuming country, by far, followed by Germany and the United Kingdom. The United States and Western Europe account for about 75 percent of cigar sales worldwide. The ratio of male to female smokers is currently four to one, but getting closer every day.

There were significant increases in cigar smoking during the 1990s and early 2000s in the United States among both adults and adolescents. Cigar usage among young adult males tripled during the 1990s. One theory is that proliferation of the many glossy magazines extolling the virtues of the cigar experience caused the increase, while another theory is that a large number of celebrities are regularly shown smoking cigars. Whatever.

Today, production is up, quality is first-rate, and the cigar and cigar smoking flourish, more popular than ever.

Chapter 2

SOME DEFINITIONS AND TERMS

THIS BRINGS US TO THE "EDUCATIONAL" PORTION OF OUR PROGRAM.

Most often, cigars go in your mouth. But, you might ask, what goes into cigars? The answer to this question is the absolute key to assessing the quality of a specific cigar.

So, let's start from jump.

WHAT'S IN A CIGAR?

For a product that can be extraordinarily complex, the basic makeup of cigars is fairly simple.

All cigars include three elements:

1. The filler tobacco at the center.

2. A binder leaf, which holds the filler together.

3. The outer wrapper, which is rolled around the binder. Besides providing a cleaner, smoother look, these are the higher quality leaves.

Cigars that are made by hand use *long filler* tobacco, leaves that run the length of a cigar. In a handmade, the filler, binder, and wrapper are combined manually.

George Burns

Machine-made cigars utilize high-speed machinery to combine *short filler* tobacco—usually scraps or pieces of tobacco leaves—or a mixed filler of long and short pieces with a binder and wrapper. Because of the tension placed on the tobacco by the machines, the binders and wrappers are often made of homogenized tobacco leaf products, stronger than natural leaves and produced in a variety of flavors, strengths, and textures.

A *puro* is a cigar that is made entirely from the tobacco of one country. It is rare to find these today and when you do, you'll pay a premium price.

There is an age-old argument—one that rages on about the differences between handmade cigars and machine-made ones. Pay no mind. Handmade is always best.

They're made with great care; they're usually made to order, and by people with a discerning eye that can choose the best tobacco needed to make them.

CHOOSING A CIGAR

TELLING THE DIFFERENCE

There are three basic qualities to apply to the process of choosing the right cigar for yourself: size, shape, and color. While all that really matters at the end of this is your picking the cigars that you like and make you happy, you should really know this stuff.

Here are the general rules of thumb.

Size

"Size matters!"

Yeah, well that's true for a lot of things. But not, for the most part, for cigars.

There are two components that make up the classifications of size in cigars: length and ring gauge. Cigars distributed in the United States have the length noted in inches, and ring gauge is noted in sixty-fourths of an inch. For example, a cigar that has a 50-ring gauge is 50/64 of an inch.

The definition of *short* is less than 5.5 inches. *Long* is greater than 6.5 inches. *Thin* is less than 42 ring size while *thick* is greater than 47 ring size.

In cigars, it typically all comes down to one's taste preferences. After that, deciding factors include the circumstances that need to be considered, like the length of time you have to smoke or whether you're celebrating something.

One general rule to follow is that the wider the cigar, the more full-bodied it will be. Longer cigars tend to smoke cooler, while the short cigars, Petite Coronas for instance, tend to burn hotter.

Experiment. Try out different sizes and make your choice. Much of the fun is in trying new types and new brands.

Here's an easy chart:

Name	Length	Ring Gauge
Corona	5½" to 6"	42 to 45
Panatela	5½" to 6½"	34 to 38

Lonsdale	6" to 6½"	42 to 44
Churchill	6½" to 7"	46 to 48
Robusto	4½" to 5"	48 to 50
Toro	6" to 6½"	48 to 50
Presidente	7" to 8½"	52 to 60
Torpedo (cone-shaped head)	5½" to 6½"	46 to 52

Shape

The definitions used in cigars for "shapes" are based on two areas: the classic definitions used in early development for Cuban cigars and the universal language used by the many cigar manufacturers. It can be confusing. You can refer to a cigar as a shape when you really mean a size and vice versa. Don't panic. Use this as a gauge.

Most cigars are shaped like a cylinder and are generally divided into *parejos* and *figurados*.

A parejo is any straight-sided cigar with no change in width and a flat head. Everything else is a figurado, or a cigar with an irregular shape.

Put them together and you get *vitolas,* a Spanish word that is basically the technical term to describe the appearance of all cigars. And while *vitola* is the given name for a size and shape of a cigar, it can also be used to refer to the band as a method of description. Here's a list of the most popular cigar shapes:

Vitolas

- Corona: 5½" x 42—The standard cigar size, and basis for all other cigar sizes.

- Petite Corona: 5" x 42—Short version of the corona.

- Corona Gorda: 5½" x 46—Fatter version of the corona; sometimes called the corona extra.

- Double Corona: 7¾" x 49—Extra long, fat version of the standard corona.

- Lonsdale: 6 ½" x 42—Longer version of a corona.

- Robusto: 5" x 50—One of the most popular sizes today, which wasn't made until a few decades ago.

- Toro: 5" x 50—Longer version of a robusto.

- Churchill: 7" x 47—Longer and slightly thinner than a toro.

- 6" x 60—A fairly new size without a standardized name. Sometimes called a *toro extra* or *gigante*.

- Lancero: 7½" x 38—A vitola that faded in popularity, but has soared back in the past couple of years.

Figurados

- Torpedo: 6½" x 52—Roughly toro-sized vitola with a pointed head; length and sharpness of the point vary greatly among brands.

- Pyramid: 7" x 56—The pyramid is different from the torpedo in that it flares out at the end like the name implies; lots of manufacturers and smokers use this interchangeably with the torpedo.

- Belicoso: 5½" x 50—Shorter than a torpedo with a shorter, rounder head; once again, it varies among brands.

- Perfecto: Narrow at the foot and head with a bulge in the middle with no customary length or ring gauge.

- Culebra: Three short, thin cigars braided together and tied at the ends; not very many are made. These used to be given to cigar rollers in the morning as their smokes for the day.

Color

The first thing you see when you buy cigars is the color. "Color" in cigar-speak is the exterior wrapper, and it's an important part of any great smoke. Supposedly, there are over one hundred different wrapper shades but they can all be grouped under these color classifications. With a few exceptions, most of this tobacco is grown in almost every country that produces cigars.

Claro: A light tan color, practically beige. Usually Connecticut-grown or grown from Connecticut seeds.

Double claro: Sometimes referred to as *candela*; this is a green wrapper and hard to find, as it's not really grown nowadays. If you do find them, they're usually from the Dominican Republic.

Colorado: Has a reddish tint to it.

Colorado claro: Medium brown and probably the most popular color you'll find. These tobaccos are grown in a number of countries.

Maduro: Dark brown to an almost black color. Most maduro wrappers are grown in Nicaragua, Brazil, Mexico, and Connecticut. They tend to be slightly "sweeter" and are usually cured for longer periods of time.

Colorado maduro: A minuscule variation from the typical maduro, but a darker brown than the Colorado claro. Often grown from African tobacco.

Oscuro: This is jet black. Only recently started to reappear after having been scarce for decades.

Unusual Wrappers and Shapes

The renewed cigar boom has prompted many manufacturers to be creative with their marketing and many are now using multiple wrappers and unusual shapes to entice cigar buyers.

Some of the newer types:

Candy canes: Tri-colored wrappers, wrapped to look like a barber pole or candy cane.

Dual-wrapper cigars: These use layered wrappers to make an unusual taste or blend, often combining wrappers from different regions.

Shorter cigars: There has also been a trend recently to a much shorter cigar, often referred to as a "nub." It's usually a 3-inch or 4-inch cigar that is geared toward a quick smoke.

Bill Cosby

Chapter 3

HOW TO ENJOY A CIGAR

"A good cigar is like tasting a good wine: you smell it, you taste it, you look at it, you feel it—you can even hear it. It satisfies all the senses."

—ANONYMOUS

OKAY, NOW WE GET DOWN TO THE GOOD PART. YOU'RE READY TO GO OUT and make that purchase. Could be a major one, as the cost of cigars has risen steadily in the past few years. You've done your homework (read this book, of course); you've set aside some time, scoured the yellow pages, or gone online to locate that perfect store.

Let's get started.

FINDING A GREAT CIGAR STORE

This is going to be key. While there are plenty of places to get cigars (I strongly recommend you stay away from drugstores, grocery stores, convenience stores, and most bodegas unless they specialize in cigars or fine tobacco, or you're going to get stale, old, and dried-out stogies), finding a truly great store can be quite the undertaking.

Depending on where you live, you might not have convenient access to a world-class cigar seller. Obviously, the Web is a great tool, not only for finding but also for buying. However, there's nothing like a great tobacco store for a truly wonderful experience.

When you've decided on the shop (or shops) you want to try, call ahead and ask for the name of their most knowledgeable cigar person. Then make an appointment or jot down the times when that person is there.

Once in the store, describe to the salesperson (who should become your new best friend) the cigars you have had in the past, what you liked and didn't like, and the kind of taste and experience you're looking for. Don't be shy—treat the purchase of a cigar as you would any major purchase. Ask lots of questions. Smoking it will take an hour or more of your time. It's an important decision.

USING YOUR SENSES

All of your senses are required when choosing a cigar. A great rule of thumb is to trust your instincts and pick out what you think you like and what smells, feels, and looks good to you. Again, ask a *lot* of questions. Any cigar purveyor worth his salt will accommodate you. If he doesn't, find a better store.

After you've determined the size, brand, and shape you think you want to smoke, pick up a few cigars and give them what I call the squeeze test, which will let you gauge the moistness and freshness of a cigar. To do this, grasp one lightly, like you would grasp a child by the arm. But be careful—if you squeeze too hard, even the best cigar will crack. Cigar wrappers are fragile. Press the cigar gently between your thumb and index finger to test its condition. It should feel firm but springy . . . yielding and moist. It should also have what's known as *reflex*—coming back almost immediately to its original shape after a gentle squeeze.

Ask if you can sample the aroma. Smelling a cigar is frowned upon in many cigar stores, but as you establish yourself as a good customer, that will change. While smell and taste are personal distinctions, you should look for a number of aromas that identify a good cigar—spice, leather, fresh grass, chocolate, nuts . . . and some earthier smells, like cedar or manure.

The wrapper must be pleasing to your eye. Do you like the look of it? Make sure there are no cracks and that the shape is fairly uniform. Does the color seem even? Is there a light sheen to the leaf? Sheen is defined as a mild shine, although that can differ from cigar to cigar, depending on the region or country you've chosen. Did I mention that you should ask a lot of questions?

Don't worry if you see a white spot or a green patch. These are natural blemishes that occurred during the growing or curing processes. There is no effect on the quality of the smoke.

Taste can only be judged by smoking—quite a pleasing challenge when you have many different cigars to choose from. But back to one of the remaining senses; one school of thought holds that rolling the cigar near your ear enables you to "hear" the quality. I've asked a number of experts and opinions all vary widely. At the very least it can be another test for freshness.

Experiment. Start with one of the lighter flavored ones or those brands with smaller formats. If you've got a bit more experience with cigars, I can tell you that the best guide in making a purchase is often the amount of time you have to smoke it. Remember that a long-filler cigar is constructed so that its flavor will intensify by stages as it smokes down. The taste in the first third can change dramatically by the end.

It is best not to abandon a cigar before it's had the chance to become all it can be. So pick a cigar you have the time to enjoy in its entirety. You will be rewarded.

GETTING READY

Okay, you have your cigar. You're in the smoke shop or a bar or on a boat or on the beach or on your front porch. You have the time to settle down or sit back and light up and enjoy your smoke. Let's prep.

CUTTING THE CIGAR

Cutting is about airflow. The objective is simple. You must create an opening wide enough to ensure an unobstructed draw while leaving enough of the cap to stop the wrapper from unraveling. The cut should be made just above the line where the cap meets the wrapper. It sounds simple, but a bad cut can ruin a good cigar.

Take your time. And use the proper implements.

A number of tools are available for the job. The most popular design is the single- or double-bladed guillotine. Many cigar stores give these away as promotional items. Feel free to take one. However, get your own as well and spend the money for a decent one. The better ones are not that expensive and they tend to stay sharper longer.

And if money is no object, you might consider buying a pair of special cigar scissors. These are usually quite sharp and cut cleanly, but can also be costly.

Two other methods of cutting are the punch cutter, with a small circular blade, and the V-cutter, which cuts a V-shaped slice across the cap.

I don't recommend either. Even when used with care, both have a tendency to tear the cap and neither can cut cigars with pointed ends. There is also some evidence that that these cutters distort the flavor of the cigar and can concentrate the smoke, making it seem like the stick is burning hot.

And while we're on the subject, never pierce the cap with a match, a cocktail stick, or a "poker" of any kind. This compresses the filler, impedes the draw, and leaves the cigar a mess.

Finally, although the technique has been used to cool effect in countless movies (Clint Eastwood, with the cigarillo perpetually clenched between his teeth, comes to mind), never, ever bite off the end of the cigar . . . unless you're a Master Cigar Maker . . . and even then, we'd ask you to reconsider it. Even with *very* sharp teeth, you can't achieve any kind of precision and the chances of ruining the smoke are great.

Buy a cutter. They're fairly inexpensive and readily available. Or put it on your Father's Day/Christmas/birthday list. It makes a great gift—for you, and for your cigars.

Note: Recently, a new tool has appeared on the horizon called a CigarSpike. This is a small device that looks like a sharp guitar pick. These are usually attached to your key chain so you can use it in case you're somewhere without your cutter and find an opportunity to have a smoke. The one I used did a nice enough job, but I'm filing these under "only in a pinch." If you push in too much, you can crack or break the cigar. In can also cause the cigar to split at the cap as you smoke it down and the moisture starts to soften the tobacco.

The band: on or off?

This has always been an area of major debate. Ultimately, it doesn't really matter. All that matters is preference . . . and a little common sense.

The band, of course, is the decorative piece of paper usually wrapped around the head of the cigar. Its purpose is to identify the brand. Some people think leaving it on is a way of "showing off" that one is smoking an expensive cigar. Those who hold such views feel you should remove the band right away before smoking the cigar; others say to leave the band on to preserve the quality of the smoke and to keep the cigar from unraveling.

The only other reason often cited for leaving the band on is so that you don't damage the delicate wrapper leaf, because pulling the band off may tear the leaf and spoil your smoking experience. That can certainly happen.

As bands have gotten bigger, they can also impede the smoking. This is especially true with the recent movement of many companies toward using double bands.

My preference is to remove the band but keep it close, in case someone asks what you're smoking and, as it's the third cigar of the night, you may not remember. Why miss out on a possible great cigar conversation?

Or, do what wine lovers do with labels and collect 'em all. A number of great cigar journals on the market allow you to paste in and organize the bands so you can savor the memories of where, when, and what you smoked. I realize it's kind of hardcore, but going back over your journal after a period of time can help you relive some of the classic smokes you've had in the past and remind you of the brands you might want to smoke again. I've even left some pages blank at the back of this book to enable you to use this book for that purpose . . . as the keeper of the finer smokes you had that you want to remember.

A helpful hint: Most bands come off more easily after the cigar is lit and the glue warms up. Squeeze the band a little to loosen it but be careful . . . if it starts to unroll the tobacco, it can ruin a cigar quickly.

LIGHTING

This is an area where cigar smokers often tend to argue—a lot. I'm going to give you my opinions and let you be the judge.

Two basic principles apply. The first is to light your cigar with an odorless flame from a butane lighter or a wooden match. I repeat: Always use a butane gas lighter or a wooden match. Never use any lighter that uses lighter fluid, wax matches, paper matches, or a candle . . . the aromas will permeate the cigar.

The second is to take your time and do a thorough job. Nothing ruins the enjoyment of a great cigar faster than the thin smoke you draw in when it's badly lit.

Here is a small ritual to help you get it right every time:

The end you cut and smoke is called the "cap." The end you light is called the "tuck" or "foot."

Hold the foot (the open end) of the cigar at 90 degrees to the flame, about a half-inch or so away from the cigar. Try not to let the flame touch the cigar.

Next, place it in your mouth and gently repeat the process, all the time rotating the cigar. Rotation is very important.

Now take it out and look at the foot. Is it lit and burning evenly? If not, repeat the process on the uneven side until to get it where you want it.

And blow on it a little if you want. It makes a pretty color.

Once you get it lit, sit back, relax, and enjoy. It's the little things, my friends, the little things.

Note: Of late, a new method has appeared to be in vogue. Called the Spanish method, it involves not cutting the cap until after you've lit the foot. Once you have an even burn going, use your cutter to snip off the cap and draw in. The result is a more even ash and an easier burn. Try it.

THE ACTUAL SMOKING OF THE DAMNED THING

Okay, okay . . . so there are a few rules. But it'll be worth it. Promise.

A cigar should be smoked slowly.

A cigar should be smoked slowly.

A cigar should be smoked slowly.

No joke. A great cigar, like a great wine or cognac, should be sipped rather than gulped. Otherwise, it may overheat, which can harm the flavor.

Never inhale. This can be hard to remember if you're used to smoking cigarettes. Concentrate. Gently draw the smoke into your mouth and allow it to play gloriously on your taste buds.

Relax and savor the subtle flavors and aromas of the tobaccos in the blend. After a while, your palate will be able to discern all of the nuances that make this one of the finest ways in the universe to relax.

Legally.

WHEN TO STOP

You can smoke a cigar as far down as you want, as long as you're still enjoying it. Smoke it until you don't want to smoke it anymore. A great cigar will be good to the last puff.

It is fine to relight your cigar if it goes out. Tap it on the ashtray and clean off any loose ash or you may find it hard to re-ignite. And be careful if a fairly long amount of time has gone by. Sometimes, a cigar that's been out for a while will be slightly bitter and/or smoke a little harsh when you relight it.

Don't concern yourself with the length or fate of the ash. (See "Tapping That Ash" on page 28.)

After you've finished one cigar and want another (and you *will* want another) give yourself some time, at least fifteen to twenty minutes. Immediately lighting up again is considered "bad form" by other cigar smokers. A true aficionado will also savor the experience of the just-finished smoke. It's all good.

PUTTING OUT AND DISCARDING YOUR CIGAR

When you put out your cigar, do not crush it out like one would a cigarette. Beside being bad cigar etiquette, crushing it will make it smolder and can make it give off a foul smell. Just let the cigar sit in the ashtray and within a few minutes it will go out by itself. When you are finished with your cigar, it is best to discard the butt right away, as it becomes bitter and also gives off a bad odor after it sits for a while.

BASIC PROBLEM SOLVING

THE UNEVEN BURN

When you encounter the unfortunate occasion in which your cigar burns faster down one side, or runs, you need to be careful. It can become messy, with ashes falling off one side; and the falling pieces of burning wrapper can burn your clothes, carpet, or skin.

This syndrome occurs when the cigar contains construction flaws, such as improperly bunched filler leaves. Even then, you may be able to salvage your smoke. As soon as you see the cigar start to burn unevenly, let the cigar go out in your ashtray. Roll off as much ash as possible. Keep the uneven section toward the bottom if possible. Slowly and carefully burn off the unburned section. Try to even up the cigar and start smoking it again.

SPLIT OR UNRAVELING WRAPPER

If you clip your cigar too close, the wrapper may start to unravel. If this happens, lightly moisten the end of the wrapper with your tongue and wrap it back around the cigar. You may have to do this more than once during the smoke.

If you have a split wrapper, it is because the cigar was not kept properly humidified and so it dried out. This makes for an unpleasant smoke and you should probably just throw the cigar away. If you want to smoke it anyway, take the wrapper off and discard it. The cigar won't look pretty, but you will avoid the possibility of the wrapper unraveling and becoming a problem.

Splitting can also occur with a sudden change of temperature. Be careful about going outside in cold temps with a cigar straight from your humidor or with a cigar that's been humidified in a store at room temperature.

TAPPING THAT ASH

The technique of ashing involves turning rather than tapping. You don't need to tap or flick a cigar ash repeatedly like you would a cigarette.

A good handmade cigar holds an ash far longer and has an ash that's far sturdier than a cheaper machine-made cigar. Mess with the ash with too much force and you can break off the ember of the cigar, which may force you to relight. Ash and ye shall receive.

Note: There's been a trend recently toward seeing how long an ash can be held. Resist the temptation. Not only is it considered bad cigar form, the ash can fall off and burn those around you or, at the very least, make quite the mess. Don't make an ash of yourself.

KEEPING CIGARS

HUMIDORS

The purpose of a humidor is to keep your cigars at their peak "smok-ability." An entire industry exists for making humidors that help you keep your cigars nice and smokable. Special boxes, bookcases, and even entire rooms are specially designed for cigars, all with con-trolled moisture and temperature.

While most good cigar shops keep all their cigars in humidors ready for sale and in perfect condition, keeping them that way after you buy them is also a priority. I recommend that you invest in a humidor of your own to keep a selection of cigars ready to smoke once you get them home.

It's a serious purchase; the better ones can be quite expensive. But you're worth it, no?

When buying a humidor, like when buying cigars, ask a lot of questions. Is there proper air circulation? Does it maintain a constant level of humidity?

Check the construction. Are the seams perfect? Does the lid shut tightly but still allow airflow? Is the lid heavy enough? What kind of humidification device is needed?

Whatever you decide, cigars should always be kept in a controlled environment. Keep in mind that if different types of cigars are stored together in the same humidor, they often take on each other's flavors. It can get expensive to purchase a humidor for each of your favorite brands or types, so make sure your humidor has dividers.

The general rule is always to buy a humidor that's slightly bigger than you think you need. Cigars take a few days to acclimatize to the conditions inside so it is a good idea to buy a humidor with a tray that allows new arrivals to be separated from the old.

The Right Conditions

Opinions differ, but most aficionados will tell you that cigars should be stored at between 68 and 72°F and in a relative humidity of 65 to 70 percent.

The humidity is the most crucial aspect. If a cigar becomes too wet it will not smoke. If it dries out, it will taste harsh. As humidity varies with temperature changes, it is also important to keep the temperature constant.

Putting cigars in the fridge is not an alternative. Refrigerators are drier than you might think. Some cigars can also absorb the smells that are there. (Imagine a ham or chicken salad cigar.)

AGING

Many cigar lovers feel that a great cigar is one that's been aged.

Aging a cigar is a matter of personal taste. Some prefer fresh cigars, those rolled within the last six months. Others will age their cigars a full five to six years (or longer) before smoking them.

As you become a more experienced cigar enthusiast, you will begin to know the pleasures of a well-aged cigar. The subtle flavors and complex constitution of an aged cigar are similar to those of a well-aged wine.

All handmade long-filler cigars improve with aging, so before you dismiss any cigar as "bad" you should allow it to rest untouched for a while. You will be genuinely surprised how many of those poor cigars blossom into enjoyable smokes. However, aging cannot improve cigars that are made from inferior or under-cured tobacco.

DRIED-OUT CIGARS

Unfortunately, it's nearly impossible to recondition or "bring back" a cigar if it's been left unhumidified and has dried out. You can place them in your humidor for a few weeks and hope for the best, moving them around occasionally. Do not put them in your refrigerator or keep them out in the bathroom when you shower or put them wrapped up in the dishwasher. More often than not, you'll just have to bite the bullet and take the hit . . . and know better for the next time.

TAKING CIGARS ON THE ROAD

Traveling with cigars can be a tricky undertaking. Once again, it'll merit another visit to the cigar store to see what's available for cigar cases.

CIGAR CASES

The same rules apply as for purchasing a humidor. Ask questions. The case should be durable and easy to access and should fit the sizes you tend to smoke most often. A case that works best is one that is compact and portable, especially if you fly a lot. To that end, try to keep your case in your carry-on when you travel. Putting cigars in a checked bag can be a recipe for disaster, not only because of the temperature changes but also because of the possibilities for mishandling.

W.C. Fields

Chapter 4

THE BEST DRINKS TO ACCOMPANY CIGARS

"There's something about having a great bottle of wine and a great cigar. Nothing compares to it."

—D. L. HUGHLEY

"The best cigar in the world is the one you prefer to smoke on special occasions, enabling you to relax and enjoy that which gives you maximum pleasure."

—ZINO DAVIDOFF

HOW MUCH FUN WILL IT BE TESTING THE DIFFERENT COMBINATIONS until you find one that you love? A lot. While some people enjoy the traditional accompaniments of cognac or port, others prefer a single-malt scotch or a martini or a fine rum. Even coffee or tea has been known to go well with cigars. In fact, it turns out that almost any drink with a flavor complex enough can be a good match to a fine cigar.

COGNAC

Cognac is the traditional drink to have with cigars. This is largely because of timing—both were usually taken after meals, and so they naturally became linked. To some, there is no better drink to combine with a cigar after a meal.

When buying cognac, pay attention to the age designation of the bottle. VS (Very Special) cognac is the lowest category of age, and should generally be ignored for pairing with cigars. The middle age bracket is designated VSOP (Very Special Old Pale), and indicates ageing of at least four and a half years. Mild and medium-bodied cigars go particularly well with this age of cognac. The highest age bracket is XO, standing for Extra Old, and has a minimum ageing requirement of six and a half years, although much older brandies can sometimes be part of the blend. These tend to be the smoothest and can be sipped slowly with those rare and expensive cigars you splurged for on a whim . . . a whim that will play out nicely.

BOURBON AND SCOTCH

In the world of spirits, small batch and single barrel bourbons and single malt scotches are super premium products that have the complexity and depth of flavor to stand up to a cigar.

The smoky quality of a fine single malt, derived from the smoked peat used to filter the spirit, marries perfectly with a good cigar. The small batch bourbons are bottled at a higher proof level, which gives them a backbone of strong flavors, and they marry well with medium- and full-bodied cigars.

Kentucky straight bourbons and Tennessee whisky, although often a bit lighter, also mix well with cigars because of the charred wood flavors that turn the liquors dark brown.

PORT

Port is another traditional partner for a great cigar. The sweetness and alcoholic power of vintage port blends perfectly with a full-bodied smoke; even younger vintage ports are appropriate because their strong tannins stand up to a spicy smoke. Non-vintage styles such as tawny port also complement a cigar nicely because of the woody characteristics they acquire during long barrel aging.

MARTINIS

Martinis come in many, many different flavors these days but they all have one thing in common: they all contain lots of alcohol. Choose a full-bodied cigar to go with a martini.

RUM

Traditionally, rum and cigars come from a similar geographical area. Whether we are talking Cuba or the Caribbean, the people who make cigars have also made rum. For this reason, the two things complement each other very well.

The cigar makers make their cigars to go with the drink they know. This has changed somewhat in the modern world; cigar makers are not necessarily limited to drinking only rum, and thus the cigars they produce might be better suited to other drinks.

However, you should know that rum in its cheapest and most basic form can ruin even the best cigar, accentuating any roughness of the smoke until all pleasure is lost completely.

WINE

Popular wine tastings are frequently offered with pairings, usually something incredibly fabulous to eat that's been made in a five-star kitchen by some celebrity chef. However, of late, many of the finer

establishments have been experimenting with pairing wines and cigars. The most popular pairing has been with the full-bodied reds.

KAHLUA OR BAILEY'S DRINKS AND COFFEE DRINKS

These drinks actually pair nicely with cigars. With coffee drinks, there are many variations, such as the black Russian, mudslide, and nutty Irishman. The sweetness of the liqueur mellows some of the bite of the cigar.

Cappuccino, lattes, and various types of coffee such as Cuban or Brazilian also work.

Coffee with Irish cream or Bailey's can greatly enhance your cigar smoking experience.

Note: When using Bailey's, there's really no need to add sugar or cream unless you really want to know what a diabetic coma feels like.

Fidel Castro

Chapter 5

THE MYTH OF THE MYSTICAL CUBAN CIGAR

"The Cuban climate gave to tobacco grown there the best aroma in the world—and the Cubans, the most beautiful skin."

—HERMAN MELVILLE

"I just smoked a Cohiba the other day. It was great. You have to appreciate everything that cigar is."

—DAISY FUENTES

INVARIABLY, WHETHER YOU'RE AT A CIGAR BAR OR IN A CIGAR STORE OR just having a conversation about cigars, the topic always seems to turn to Cubans. "Hey, have you ever smoked any Cubans?" . . . "Can you get hold of any Cuban cigars?" . . . "What about Cuban cigars, are they that much better?"

They're not.

Wow, I can hear the screaming from here. *It was the lambs, Clarice, the lambs . . .*

First, let me say that one of my fondest memories was sitting at the Duck Pond Restaurant in the Ritz-Carlton Hotel in Montreal with my wife and two friends, after an amazing meal, finishing up with a cheese plate and the most wonderful port . . . and smoking a Cohiba Churchill that might have been the best cigar I'd ever had up to that time. I also remember it cost me almost $30 Canadian, the most money I'd ever spent on a cigar. This was 1985.

That was then and this is now.

In the last few decades, cigar manufacturing around the world has come a long way. Almost half of the cigars smoked in the United States come from the Dominican Republic. The rest hail from Nicaragua, Mexico, Honduras, and many other countries around the world, and the world's finest cigars come from places other than Cuba.

Why is that? (History lesson alert!)

Since 1962, Cuban cigars have been unavailable in the United States. Legally, that is.

This was the result of an embargo levied by President Kennedy, a commercial, economic, and financial embargo imposed on the Castro government. The government's plan was to maintain these sanctions on the Castro regime as long as it continued to refuse to move toward democratization and greater respect for human rights. Unfortunately, Fidel was just as stubborn, and to this day the embargo stands. An immovable object meets an irresistible force.

One of the more interesting aspects of the increased demand and production in the world's tobacco supply of cigars has been the reported decrease in the quality of the cigars from Cuba. In the 1990s, a number of top cigar makers announced that they would stop selling the lines of Cuban cigars for that reason. Instead, many began to tout other areas, like the Dominican Republic and Nicaragua.

Currently, U.S. law stipulates that you can only go to Cuba in three instances:

1. As a full-time journalist.
2. If your trip is being "fully hosted" and all your expenses are covered by a foreign citizen or organization that is not being reimbursed.
3. With a license for educational or religious travel, usually in a group. Getting that license can take months.

There has been a renewed effort of late to revisit the embargo question, and it looks like we may see travel to Cuba for Americans as a possibility soon. Once that happens, and there is a new influx of tourism dollars in their economy, the high quality of the smokes should return and the Cuban cigar will take its place at the top once again. Until then, there are a lot of phenomenal cigars to choose from.

Note: If you do try to get Cuban cigars, be really careful out there. There are many counterfeit "Cuban" cigars being touted in the marketplace. Recently, a major arrest was made in Florida of a group of criminals who were taking cheap domestic cigars, replacing the bands with Cuban bands, and placing them in authentic Cuban cigar boxes for sale as "Cuban cigars." Many of these made their way out into the world before the bust.

If someone makes the claim that they have "pre-embargo" cigars, ask a lot of questions and get as much proof as possible. Real pre-embargo cigars will be very expensive, although that can also be an indication of legitimacy.

Sigmund Freud

Chapter 6

THE FINE ART OF THE CIGAR QUOTE

OKAY, ENOUGH ALREADY WITH THE TECHNICAL STUFF.

Cigar lovers all tend to have one thing in common: They love talking about cigars. What was the best smoke you ever had? Who has the finest selection?

Much fun can be had in a cigar conversation, and one way to show your cigar prowess is through the use of the cigar quote. As can be seen from the many storied and prestigious folks who have been quoted here, cigars have been and remain an important part of the experience of living . . . and it seems like everyone has something to say about cigars.

CLASSIC QUOTES

If smoking is not allowed in heaven, I shall not go.

—MARK TWAIN

I didn't play at collecting. No cigar anywhere was safe from me.

—EDWARD G. ROBINSON

A woman is only a woman, but a good cigar is a smoke.

—RUDYARD KIPLING

———

Happiness? A good cigar, a good meal, a good cigar, and a good woman—or a bad woman; it depends on how much happiness you can handle.

—GEORGE BURNS

———

If I paid ten dollars for a cigar, I'd make love to it first and then smoke it.

—GEORGE BURNS

———

I smoke in moderation . . . only one cigar at a time.

—MARK TWAIN

———

I never can understand how anyone cannot smoke. It deprives a man of the best part of life. With a good cigar in his mouth a man is perfectly safe; nothing can touch him, literally.

—THOMAS MANN

———

I'm at the age now where just putting my cigar in its holder is a thrill.

—GEORGE BURNS

———

The cigar is the perfect complement to an elegant lifestyle.

—GEORGE SAND

———

Given the choice between a woman and a cigar, I will always choose the cigar.

—GROUCHO MARX

A good cigar is as great a comfort to a man as a good cry is to a woman.

—EDWARD BULWER-LYTTON

Ah, if only I had brought a cigar with me! This would have established my identity.

—CHARLES DICKENS

I drink a great deal. I sleep a little, and I smoke cigar after cigar. That is why I am in two-hundred-percent form.

—WINSTON CHURCHILL

If I had taken my doctor's advice and quit smoking when he advised me to, I wouldn't have lived to go to his funeral.

—GEORGE BURNS

There is nothing more agreeable than having a place where one can throw on the floor as many cigar butts as one pleases without the subconscious fear of a maid who is waiting like a sentinel to place an ashtray where the ashes are going to fall.

—FIDEL CASTRO

My rule of life prescribed as an absolutely sacred rite smoking cigars and also the drinking of alcohol before, after, and if need be during all meals and in the intervals between them.

—WINSTON CHURCHILL

My boy! Smoking is one of the greatest and cheapest enjoyments in life, and if you decide in advance not to smoke, I can only feel sorry for you.

—SIGMUND FREUD TO HIS YOUNG NEPHEW AFTER HE DECLINED A CIGAR

There are men here and there to whom the whole of life is like an after-dinner hour with a cigar; easy, pleasant, empty, perhaps enlivened by some fable of strife to be forgotten before the end is told—even if there happens to be any end to it.

—JOSEPH CONRAD

I owe to my cigar a great intensification of my capacity to work and a facilitation of my self-control.

—SIGMUND FREUD

Little tube of mighty pow'r, charmer of an idle hour, object of my warm desire.

—ISAAC HAWKINS BROWNE

Lastly (and this is, perhaps, the golden rule), no woman should marry a man who does not smoke.

—ROBERT LOUIS STEVENSON

To cease smoking is the easiest thing I ever did. I ought to know because I've done it a thousand times.

—MARK TWAIN

I have met many alchemists who have let gold go up in smoke, but only you, Sir Walter, have I seen transmute smoke into gold.

—ELIZABETH I

You should hurry up and acquire the cigar habit. It's one of the major happinesses. And so much more lasting than love, so much less costly in emotional wear and tear.

—ALDOUS HUXLEY

Women are jealous of cigars . . . they regard them as a strong rival.

—WILLIAM MAKEPEACE THACKERAY

Smoking is indispensable if one has nothing to kiss.

—SIGMUND FREUD

He who doth not smoke hath either known no great griefs, or refuseth himself the softest consolation, next to that which comes from heaven.

—EDWARD GEORGE BULWER-LYTTON

Great unaccredited cigar quotes

Cigar smoking knows no politics. It's about the pursuit of pleasure, taste, and aroma.

Some men smoke between meals; other men eat between smokes.

A good cigar is like tasting a good wine: you smell it, you taste it, you look at it, you feel it—you can even hear it. It satisfies all the senses.

To smoke is human; to smoke cigars is divine.

As you approach thirty, you have a thirty-ring gauge; as you approach fifty, you have a fifty-ring gauge.

—CUBAN SAYING

Allah made tobacco grow to put a smile on the faces of men.

—TURKISH PROVERB

The most futile and disastrous day seems well spent when it is reviewed through the blue, fragrant smoke of a Havana cigar.

—EVELYN WAUGH

———

Do not ask me to describe the charms of reverie, or the contemplative ecstasy into which the smoke of our cigar plunges us.

—JULES SANDEAU

———

By the cigars they smoke, and the composers they love, ye shall know the texture of men's souls.

—JOHN GALSWORTHY

———

Cigars after dinner are delightful; before breakfast is unnatural.

—GEORGE BERNARD SHAW

———

On a cold winter morning a cigar fortifies the soul.

—STENDHAL

———

For undemocratic reasons and for motives not of State, they arrive at their conclusions largely inarticulate. Being void of self-expression they confide their views to none; but sometimes in a smoking room, one learns why things were done.

—RUDYARD KIPLING

———

A cigar is the perfect type of a perfect pleasure. It is exquisite, and it leaves one unsatisfied. What more can one want?

—OSCAR WILDE

———

The believing we do something when we do nothing is the first illusion of tobacco.

—RALPH WALDO EMERSON

———

It has always been my rule never to smoke when asleep, and never to refrain when awake.

—MARK TWAIN

———

Lady Bracknell: "Do you smoke"?
Earnest: "Well, yes, I must admit I smoke."
Lady Bracknell: "I am glad to hear it. A man should always have an occupation of some kind."

—OSCAR WILDE'S *THE IMPORTANCE OF BEING EARNEST*

———

Don Juan took out a Seville cigar and called for a light when meeting the devil, who was traveling along the opposite bank of the river Guadalquivir.

—DON JUAN

———

A cigar has a fire at one end and a fool at the other.

—HORACE GREELEY

———

Any cigar smoker is a friend because I know how he feels.

—ALFRED DE MUSSET

———

The cigar numbs sorrow and fills the solitary hours with a million gracious images.

—GEORGE SAND

———

If a woman knows a man's preferences, including his preference in cigars, and if a man knows what a woman likes, they will be suitably armed to face one another.

—COLETTE

———

Divine in hookas, glorious in a pipe. When tipp'd with amber, mellow, rich and ripe: Yet thy true lovers more admire by far Thy naked beauties—give me a cigar!

—LORD BYRON

(Just Cuz They're Funny)

Thank you for Not Smoking. Cigar smoke is the residue of your pleasure. It contaminates the air, pollutes my hair and clothes, not to mention my lungs. This takes place without my consent. I have a pleasure, also. I like a beer now and then. The residue of my pleasure is urine. Would you be annoyed if I stood on a chair and pissed on your head and your clothes without your consent?
—SIGN FROM KEN'S MAGIC SHOP

If we see you smoking we will assume you are on fire and take appropriate action. —DOUGLAS ADAMS

Ods me I marle what pleasure or felicity they have in taking their roguish tobacco. It is good for nothing but to choke a man, and fill him full of smoke and embers. —BEN JONSON

The best way to stop smoking is to just stop—no ifs, ands, or butts. —EDITH ZITTLER

Smoke and be silent; there's only wind and smoke in the world.
—IRISH PROVERB

Cigar smoking actively encouraged.

—SIGN IN A LONDON RESTAURANT

A fine cigar is like a fine woman. They come in all shapes and sizes. Treat them tenderly and lovingly. Caress their skin, admire their beauty, and fondle them with reverence. Bring them slowly to your lips, enjoy their flavor, their aroma. Contemplate their essence, their dependability, and forgive them their weaknesses—if there be any. Revel in the rituals, their simplicity and their enduring meanings. Do these things, my son, and the blessings of life shall always be upon you.

—PRINCE SINED YAR MAHARG

I'm glad I don't have to explain to a man from Mars why each day I set fire to dozens of rolled pieces of paper, and put them in my mouth.

—MIGNON McLAUGHLIN'S
THE SECOND NEUROTIC'S NOTEBOOK

I haven't been sick a day since I was a child. A steady diet of cigars and whiskey cured me.

—W. C. FIELDS

While smoking a cigar, we are in the presence of eternity. The tobacco reminds us of the earth, from which it and we came.

As with ourselves, the life of some cigars are short, while others last a while longer, but in the end all are consumed. But the smoke, ah, the smoke! The smoke drifts gently heavenward on its quest to combine with the great eternal oneness.

—PRINCE SINED YAR MAHARG

Good food, good sex, good digestion, and good sleep: to these basic animal pleasures, man has added nothing but the good cigar.

—MIGNON MCLAUGHLIN'S
THE SECOND NEUROTIC'S NOTEBOOK

Watching the smoke dance out of a cigar is like watching a girl dance out of her dress.

—D. H. MONDFLEUR

Tobacco, divine, rare superexcellent tobacco, which goes far beyond all panaceas, potable gold and philosopher's stones, a sovereign remedy to all diseases.

—ROBERT BURTON'S *ANATOMY OF MELANCHOLY*

Coffee and tobacco are complete repose.

—TURKISH PROVERB

Still unaccredited, still funny

Please don't throw your cigar butts in the urinal. It makes them soggy and hard to light.

The cigar does the smoking—you're just the sucker.

It is difficult to be bad-tempered with a good cigar in one's mouth.

Department of Health Services warning: Nicotine patches are great. Stick one over each eye and you can't find your smokes.

If you must smoke, take your butt outside.

The best way to stop smoking is to carry wet matches.

CONTEMPORARY QUOTES

Cigarettes are for chain-smoking; cigars must be smoked one at a time, peaceably, with all the leisure in the world. Cigarettes are of the instant; cigars are for eternity.

—G. CABERA INFANTE

The only way to break a bad habit was to replace it with a better habit.

—JACK NICHOLSON

A good cigar is like a beautiful chick with a great body that also knows the American League box scores.

—KLINGER ON M*A*S*H

I kissed my first girl and smoked my first cigar on the same day. I haven't had time for tobacco since.

—ARTURO TOSCANINI

Tobacco and alcohol are delicious fathers of abiding friendships and fertile reveries.

—LUIS BUÑUEL

If your wife doesn't like the aroma of your cigar, change your wife.

—ZINO DAVIDOFF

The cigar, like the pipe, ought to match your physique.

—KEES VAN DONGEN

Remember that silence and a good cigar are two of the finest things on earth.

—JOHN BAIN

It (Love) is like a cigar. If it goes out, you can light it again but it never tastes quite the same.

—LORD WAVELL

———

Maybe it's like becoming one with the cigar. You lose yourself in it; everything fades away: your worries, your problems, and your thoughts. They fade into the smoke, and the cigar and you are at peace.

—RAUL JULIA

———

A cigar ought not to be smoked solely with the mouth, but with the hand, the eyes, and with the spirit.

—ZINO DAVIDOFF

———

Come in here, dear boy, have a cigar. You're gonna go far.
—FROM "HAVE A CIGAR," BY PINK FLOYD
(I STILL HAVE NO IDEA WHICH ONE IS PINK)

———

A cigar is as good as the memories that you have when you smoked it.

—RAUL JULIA

———

After a truly good meal, an outstanding cigar is still the most satisfying after-dinner activity that doesn't involve two human beings.

—BRAD SHAW

———

What this country needs is a really good five-cent cigar.
—THOMAS RILEY MARSHALL,
VICE PRESIDENT UNDER WOODROW WILSON

Our country has plenty of good five-cent cigars, but the trouble is they charge fifteen cents for them.

—WILL ROGERS

There's something luxurious about having a girl light your cigar. In fact, I got married once on account of that.

—HAROLD ROBBINS

I thought I couldn't afford to take her out and smoke as well. So I gave up cigars. Then I took her out and one day I looked at her and thought: "Oh well," and went back to smoking again and that was better.

—BENNY HILL

A cigar, said the altruist, a cigar, my good man, I cannot give you. But any time you need a light, just come around; mine is always lit.

—KARL KRAUS

Young man, you may or may not have murdered a middle-aged woman, but you've certainly saved the life of an elderly barrister.

—CHARLES LAUGHTON, THANKING TYRONE POWER FOR SNEAKING HIM A CIGAR IN *WITNESS FOR THE PROSECUTION*

No cigar-smoker ever committed suicide.

—WILLIAM MAGINN

I even smoke in bed. Imagine smoking a cigar in bed, reading a book. Next to your bed, there's a cigar table with a special cigar ashtray, and your wife is reading a book on how to save the environment.

—RAUL JULIA

I've got a great cigar collection—it's actually not a collection, because that would imply I wasn't going to smoke every last one of 'em.

—RON WHITE

I have to laugh when I think of the first cigar, because it was probably just a bunch of rolled up tobacco leaves.

—JACK HANDY

Why pay $100 for a therapy session when you can spend $25 on a cigar? Whatever it is will come back; so what, smoke another one.

—RAUL JULIA

I did the cover of Cigar Aficionado, *so I'm supposed to talk about loving cigars. I've smoked them a couple of times. My father used to smoke cigars. I love the idea and the concept, and I love the smell of cigars.*

—GINA GERSHON

You better take advantage of the good cigars. You don't get much else in that job.

—THOMAS P. "TIP" O'NEILL,
ADVICE TO VICE PRESIDENT WALTER MONDALE

The cigar embodies the eternal attributes of prestige, success, and savoir-faire.

—ITALO CALVINO

To fully appreciate fine cigars, it's important to recognize the various types of cigars. There are two basic categories of cigar. The lit and unlit.

—P. MARTIN SHOEMAKER

A youth with his first cigar makes himself sick; a youth with his first girl makes other people sick.

—MARY WILSON LITTLE

I can't stand cigarette smoke. . . . Cigarette smoking is both expensive and unhealthy. Now take the cigar. Cigars are an expression of the fundamental idea of smoking, both a stimulant and a relaxation. A manly vice.

—VICTOR SJOSTROM

The cigar is a great resource. It is necessary to have traveled for a long time on a ship to understand that at least the cigar affords you the pleasure of smoking. It raises your spirits. Are you troubled by something? The cigar dissolves it. Are you subject to aches and pains (or bad temper)? The cigar will change your disposition. Are you harassed by unpleasant thoughts? Smoking a cigar puts one in a frame of mind to dispense with these. Do you ever feel a little faint from hunger? A cigar satisfies the yearning. If you are obsessed by sad thoughts, a cigar will take your mind off of them. Finally, don't you sometimes have some unpleasant remembrance or consoling thought? A cigar will reinforce this. Sometimes they die out, and happy are those who do not need to relight too quickly. I hardly need to say anything more about the cigar, to which I dedicate this little eulogy for past services rendered.

—THE DUC DE LA ROCHEFOUCAULD-LIANCOURT

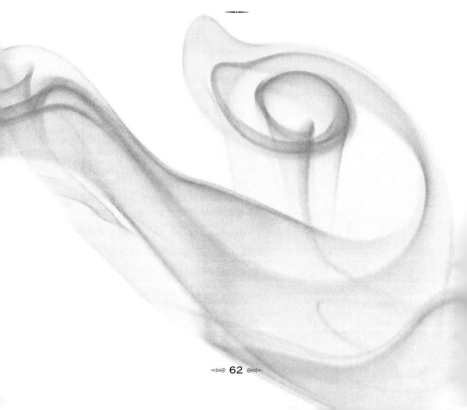

Chapter 7

THE CIGAR IN POETRY

FROM CLASSIC POETRY TO ROCK AND ROLL, CIGARS HAVE ALWAYS inspired verse. A collection of some of the best . . .

SONNET ON TOBACCO

It's all one thing—both tend into one scope—To live upon Tobacco and on Hope, The one's but smoke, the other is but wind.

—SIR ROBERT AYTOUN OF KINCALDIE

When Fear and Care and grim Despair;
Flock round me in a ghostly crowd;
One charm dispels them all in air;
I blow my after-dinner cloud.

—HENRY LEIGH

Arnold Schwarzenegger

THE CIGAR

I do not seek for fame
A general with a scar;
A private let me be,
So I have my cigar . . .
Some sigh for this or that,
My wishes don't go far;
The world may wag at will,
So I have my cigar.

—THOMAS HOOD

He sat at the Algonquin, smoking a cigar. A coffin of a clock bonged out the time. She was ten minutes late. But in that time, He puffed the blue eternity of his cigar.

—UNKNOWN

Life's a cigar: the wasting body glows; The head turns white as Kosciusko's snows; And, with the last soul-fragrance still in air, The ashes slowly sink in soft repose.

—GEORGE G. McCRAE

THE SCENT OF A GOOD CIGAR

What is it that comes through the deepening dusk,
Something sweeter than jasmine scent,
Sweeter than rose and violet blent,
More potent in power than orange or musk?
The scent of a good cigar.

I am all alone in my quiet room,
And the windows are open wide and free
To let in the south wind's kiss for me,
While I rock in the softly gathering gloom,

And that subtle fragrance steals,
Just as a loving, tender hand
Will sometimes steal in yours,
It softly comes through the open doors,
And memory wakes at its command,
The scent of that good cigar.

And what does it say?
Ah! That's for me and my heart alone to know;
But that heart thrills with a sudden glow,
Tears fill my eyes till I cannot see,
From the scent of that good cigar.

—KATE A. CARRINGTON

THE BETROTHED

"You must choose between me and your cigar."

Open the old cigar-box, get me a Cuba stout, for things are running crossways, and Maggie and I are out.

We quarreled about Havanas—we fought o'er a good cheroot, and I knew she is exacting, and she says I am a brute.

Open the old cigar-box—let me consider a space; in the soft blue veil of the vapor musing on Maggie's face.

Maggie is pretty to look at—Maggie's a loving lass, but the prettiest cheeks must wrinkle, the truest of loves must pass.

There's peace in a Larranaga, there's calm in a Henry Clay; but the best cigar in an hour is finished and thrown away—

Thrown away Maggie for fear o' the talk o' the town!

Maggie, my wife at fifty—grey and dour and old—With never another Maggie to purchase for love or gold!

And the light of Days that have Been the dark of the Days that Are, And Love's torch stinking and stale, like the butt of a dead cigar—

The butt of a dead cigar you are bound to keep in your pocket—With never a new one to light tho' it's charred and black to the socket!

Open the old cigar-box—let me consider a while. Here is a mild Manila—there is a wifely smile.

Which is the better portion—bondage bought with a ring, or a harem of dusky beauties, fifty tied in a string?

Counselors cunning and silent—comforters true and tried, and never a one of the fifty to sneer at a rival bride?

Thought in the early morning, solace in time of woes, Peace in the hush of the twilight, balm ere my eyelids close,

This will the fifty give me, asking naught in return, With only a Suttee's passion—to do their duty and burn.

This will the fifty give me. When they are spent and dead, Five times other fifties shall be my servants instead.

The furrows of far-off Java, the isles of the Spanish Main, when they hear my harem is empty will send me my brides again.

I will take no heed to their raiment, nor food for their mouths withal, So long as the gulls are nesting, so long as the showers fall.

I will scent 'em with best vanilla, with tea will I temper their hides, and the Moor and the Mormon shall envy who read of the tale of my brides.

For Maggie has written a letter to give me my choice between the wee little whimpering Love and the great god Nick o' Teen.

And I have been servant of Love for barely a twelvemonth clear, but I have been Priest of Cabanas a matter of seven year;

And the gloom of my bachelor days is flecked with the cheery light of stumps that I burned to Friendship and Pleasure and Work and Fight.

And I turn my eyes to the future that Maggie and I must prove, But the only light on the marshes is the Will-o'-the-Wisp of Love.

Will it see me safe through my journey or leave me bogged in the mire? Since a puff of tobacco can cloud it, shall I follow the fitful fire?

Open the old cigar-box—let me consider anew—Old friends, and who is Maggie that I should abandon you?

A million surplus Maggies are willing to bear the yoke; and a woman is only a woman, but a good Cigar is a Smoke.

Light me another Cuba—I hold to my first-sworn vows. If Maggie will have no rival, I'll have no Maggie for Spouse!

—RUDYARD KIPLING

TO MY CIGAR

Yes, social friend, I love thee well, In learned doctor's spite; I love thy
fragrant, misty spell, I love thy calm delight.

What if they tell, with phizzes long, Our years are sooner past? I
would reply, with reason strong, They're sweeter while they last.

And oft, mild tube, to me thou art, A monitor, though still; Thou
speak'st a lesson to my heart, Beyond the preacher's skill.

When, in the lonely evening hour, Attended but by thee, O'er hist'ry's
varied page I pore, Man's fate in thee I see.

Awhile like thee the hero burns, And smokes and fumes around, And
then like thee to ashes turns, And mingles with the ground.

Throu't like the man of worth, who gives To goodness every day, The
fragrance of whose virtues lives, When he has passed away.

Oh when thy snowy column grows, And breaks and fails away, I trace
how mighty realms thus rise, Then tumbled to decay.

From beggar's frieze to monarch's robe, One common doom is pass'd:
Sweet nature's works, the mighty globe, Must all burn out at last.

And what is he who smokes thee now? A little moving heap: That's
soon, like thee, to fate must bow, Like thee in dust must sleep.

And when I see thy smoke roll high, Thy ashes downward go,
Methinks 'tis thus my soul shall fly, Thus leave my body too.

A huge Cigar are all mankind, And time's the wasting breath, That,
late or early, we shall find, Gives all to dusty death.

—CHARLES SPRAGUE

Chapter 8

ANECDOTES

MUCH LIKE IN VERSE AND IN QUOTATION, THE LORE AROUND CIGARS IS plentiful. These are great cigar stories. True. Untrue. Doesn't matter.

During the Nazi blitz of London in 1941, one of the Luftwaffe's raids destroyed the Dunhill tobacco shop on Drake Street, in which was stored a portion of the Prime Minister **Winston Churchill**'s treasured cache of Havanas. The store manager made a careful survey of the damage and rushed to the phone to report, "Your cigars are safe, sir."

———

Thomas Edison played many a practical joke upon his employees, and in the early phonograph days, he enjoyed many a laugh on them with the aid of his "talking machine." Sometimes the joke was on him.

Edison was always an inveterate smoker, and used to keep a number of boxes of cigars in his room. These were a constant object of interest to his associates. First one man, then another, would enter the room, ask Edison some trivial question, and when leaving would manage, unseen, to insert his hand in one of the boxes and take three or four choice cigars. Edison began to suspect something of the kind, and one day he called on his tobacconist, explained what was

John
Kennedy

happening, and got the man to fix up some fearful "smokes," consisting of old bits of rag, tea leaves, and shavings, and worth about two dollars a barrel. These were done up in attractive-looking boxes, and delivered to the laboratory. Nothing happened, however; there was a falling off in the number of Edison's visitors, but no casualties were reported. Then one day Edison again called at the store, and inquired of his dealer if he had forgotten to send up the fake cigars. "Why Mr. Edison," replied the amazed tobacconist, "I sent you ten boxes of the worst concoctions that I could make two months ago. Aren't your men through with them yet?"

Edison made a rapid calculation, divided the number of cigars by his daily allowance, and was forced to conclude that he had consumed those "life destroyers" himself. There and then he gave a big order for his usual brand, and his cigars disappeared once more with their accustomed celerity.

———

On **Groucho Marx**'s 1950s TV quiz show *You Bet Your Life*, a female contestant said that the reason she had twenty-two kids was "because I love children, and I think that's our purpose here on Earth, and I love my husband." To which Groucho supposedly replied: "I love my cigar, too, but I take it out of my mouth once in a while." *[Author's note: There's lots of controversy over this one. Most Groucho scholars say he never said it, that it's been attributed to him but can't be found on any documentation or film of the show. Doesn't matter . . . it's a Groucho line in spirit.]*

———

In mid-century, Cuban cigar rollers became well versed in the classics because the cigar factories would employ readers to read aloud from literary works. **Victor Munoz,** a journalist who established Mother's Day as a holiday, was one such reader.

—·—

Franz Liszt, the Hungarian composer who, before entering a monastery for the remainder of his life, secured permission to smoke his cigars. He also traveled with an exceedingly large humidor.

—·—

A Charlotte, North Carolina, man, having purchased a box of twenty-four rare and very expensive cigars, insured them against . . . fire. Within a month, having smoked his entire stockpile of fabulous cigars, and having yet to make a single premium payment on the policy, the man filed a claim against the insurance company.

In his claim, the man stated that he had lost the cigars in "a series of small fires." The insurance company refused to pay, citing the obvious reason: that the man had consumed the cigars in a normal fashion. The man sued, and won.

In delivering his ruling, the judge stated that the man held a policy from the company in which it was warranted that the cigars were insurable.

The company, in the policy, had also guaranteed that it would insure the cigars against fire, without defining what it considered to be "unacceptable fire," and so, the company was obligated to compensate the insured for his loss.

Rather than endure a lengthy and costly appeal process, the insurance company accepted the judge's ruling and paid the man $15,000 for the rare cigars he had lost in "the fires."

However, shortly after the man cashed his check, the insurance company had him arrested on twenty-four counts of arson. With his insurance claim and the testimony from the previous case used as evidence against him, the man was convicted of intentionally burning the rare cigars and sentenced to twenty-four consecutive one-year prison terms.

———

Annie Oakley smoked small cigars, cheroots, before each shooting exhibit, claiming it calmed her nerves.

———

One evening **Winston Churchill** impulsively decided to cancel his last scheduled appointment, a visit from a tiresome diplomat who always overstayed his welcome. "When he arrives, tell him I'm out," Churchill instructed his valet, before adding, after a moment's thought, "And to convince him, smoke one of my cigars when you open the door."

———

During **World War II,** reports of the Allied naval movements, sent by German spies, were encoded to look like invoices for Havana cigars.

———

Ernest Hemingway presented Ava Gardner a cigar band as a souvenir of their first meeting, on the set of *The Sun Also Rises*—a romantic gesture made more so as he gave it to her at the bullfights.

John Wayne had special cigars made for him, larger than anything else available, so they would stand out when he smoked in his movies.

When astronaut **John Glenn** came back from piloting America's historic first orbital Mercury flight, he was given the equivalent of his weight in Havana cigars.

During the reign of Queen Victoria, smoking was frowned upon and not allowed at court. That changed when **Edward VII** came to the throne at the beginning of the twentieth century, and after dinner pronounced, "Gentlemen, you may now smoke."

In the mid-1950s, **Bob Wolff** became the voice of Madison Square Garden. "The reason I got the job," Wolff once recalled, "is that the cigar sponsor and others said to the Garden, 'You got to hire this guy; he can sell anything—not well, but he tries.'

"My first night at Madison Square Garden, they let me ad-lib the cigar ads. The big commercial was the Robert Burns Imperial, which was twenty-five cents, their top-of-the-line cigar in that glass tube. They told me to talk about its aroma—the smell of that fresh tobacco—and I'll never forget looking in the camera, the cigar under my nose, and saying, 'Boy, this has a wonderful fragrance and aroma. And what rich tobacco!'

"The telephones start ringing and the vice president of the ad agency said, 'Congratulations, those words were great. I have just one suggestion. The next time you're talking about that cigar and its wonderful aroma, please take it out of the glass tube first.'"

———

Groucho Marx used to tell this story about traveling the country. "Because we were a kid act, we traveled at half-fare, despite the fact that we were all around twenty. Our mother insisted we were thirteen. She was once stopped by a train conductor and told, 'That kid of yours is in the dining car smoking a cigar and another one is in the washroom shaving.' Minnie shook her head sadly. 'They grow so fast!'"

———

George Burns, famed for his love of fine cigars, was a longtime member of L.A.'s exclusive Hillcrest Country Club. When Burns complained one day about the club's new ban on smoking, a special sign was posted for Burns' benefit: "Cigar smoking prohibited for anyone under ninety-five."

———

Wizard of Oz creator **L. Frank Baum,** whose weak heart prevented him from smoking, often held an unlit cigar in his mouth for consolation. One day while visiting the lakeshore, Baum was asked whether he ever lit his stogies. "I only light up when I go swimming," he replied. "I can't swim, so when the cigar goes out I know I'm getting out of my depth."

By way of demonstration, he then lit the cigar, walked into the lake until the water level reached his mouth (and extinguished the cigar), and promptly returned to the shore. "There, now," he said with a smile, "if it hadn't been for the cigar I would have drowned."

———

Yousuf Karsh was a journeyman photographer who became a star when he got a chance opportunity in December 1941 to photograph Winston Churchill, who was on a brief visit to Ottawa (where Karsh was then living).

As Karsh was setting up his equipment in a room in the Canadian Parliament, Churchill was led in, grumbling. "Why was I not told of this?" he growled, lighting a cigar and offering Karsh two minutes—and no more—to take his picture.

Karsh was in a bind. Such an uncooperative subject was unlikely to produce a stellar photograph. What would he do?

Without warning, he politely but decisively plucked the smoldering cigar from Churchill's lips. "Forgive me, sir," he said, releasing the shutter on his camera—and immortalizing Churchill's scowl and determination.

—

Milton Berle sat down at the comedians' Round Table at the Hillcrest Country Club next to George Burns, who was polluting the atmosphere at the table with one of his cheap stogies (which he got for free from the Consolidated Cigar Company for which he worked).

Unable to stand the odor any longer, Berle finally turned to Burns. "You must be smoking one of those Lawrence Welk cigars," he complained. "What's a Lawrence Welk cigar?" Burns asked, reverting to his days as Gracie Allen's straight man. "A piece of s---," Berle replied, "with a band around it!"

—

Colette's advice to women on presenting a man with a fine cigar:

A woman should always keep cigars at 70 percent humidity unless she has an ulterior motive—in which case she should leave it out for a day. Then she should cry, "Oh! How careless of me," snip it, lick it gently all over and run the tip of a flame up and down its length before presenting it to the gentleman in question.

—

When **Mark Twain** married in 1870, he made a determined effort to quit smoking—and found himself quite unable to write the book he had been commissioned to write (aptly entitled *Roughing It*). "I was three weeks writing six chapters," he later recalled. "Then I gave up the fight, resumed my three hundred cigars [per month], burned the six chapters, and wrote the book in three months, without any bother."

———

One evening while dining at Legal Seafood in Boston, **Red Auerbach** was approached by a waitress who had noticed his trademark cigar. "Sorry, sir," she said, "no smoking." Auerbach smiled and directed her to look at the menu. She did so—and was amused to see a notice, which read: "No cigar or pipe smoking, except for Red Auerbach."

———

Melvin Laird, secretary under Nixon, pocketed his cigar on meeting the pope so as not to offend. His jacket caught on fire.

———

Napoleon III was asked to ban cigars and replied that he would forbid the smoking of cigars immediately, once a new source of revenue was found to replace the $100 million in tax revenue they brought in. Cigars stayed.

———

The longest cigar ever hand rolled was by **Wallace and Margarita Reyes** of Ybor City, Florida, in 2009, according to the *Guinness Book of World Records*. The cigar was 196 feet, 3⅜ inches long.

———

Christian Mortensen, known at the time of his death in 1998 as the world's oldest man, lived to the ripe old age of 115. While he preferred a vegetarian diet, one of his guilty pleasures was a fine Danish cigar, which he smoked every day. Mazel tov.

———

The message to his comrades to begin the revolution against Spanish rule was sent by the Cuban revolutionary **Jose Marti** wrapped in a cigar.

———

Cigar boxes are widely used by most jugglers in their routines. In 1977, **Kris Kremo** set a Guinness World Record by releasing one cigar box and catching it after a quadruple pirouette. Taking a turn, this record was broken years later in 1994 when **Kristian Kristof** went two steps higher and broke the record by releasing three cigar boxes and catching them after a quadruple pirouette.

———

The world record for most cigar boxes stacked: 211 boxes on top of one another, a feat that lasted for 9 seconds.

———

Babe Ruth, playing for the Boston Red Sox, loved cigars so much he became a major investor in a cigar company that made a five-cent cigar with his image on the band.

Bill Clinton

Chapter 9

CIGAR JOKES

AUTHOR'S NOTE: *ALL JOKES ARE JUST VARIATIONS OF OTHER JOKES.* There are probably ten original jokes in all. These are a handful of jokes using the cigar—to great effect.

A man walks into a dimly lit bar and the bartender asks him, "Why is the front of your shirt all bloody?"

His customer answers in a slurred voice, "My wife caught me with another woman and cut off my penis."

"Oh come on," replies the bartender.

The customer then says, "If you don't believe me, I'll show you."

He proceeds to rifle through his suitcase and pulls out this long thin thing and lays it on the bar.

The bartender bends down and looks closely and says, "Why, this is just a cigar."

The customer looks puzzled and says, "I have it here somewhere." He fumbles through his pockets and comes up with another long thin thing and places it on the bar, and says, "See that?"

The bartender again inspects it closely and says, " Idiot, that's just another cigar."

The customer staggers backward and steadies himself, leaning on the bar, and with awareness in his shaky voice says, "Son of a bitch, I must have smoked it!"

—·—

What do you get if you cross Lorena Bobbit and Monica Lewinsky?

A cigar cutter.

—·—

The druggist approached a customer who had just lit a cigar. "Excuse me," he said, "But you can't smoke in here."

The irate customer puffed a stream of smoke from the side of his mouth. "Like hell I can't! I just bought the damn thing here!"

"Big deal," replied the druggist. "We sell condoms here too."

—·—

A guy walks into a bar and sees a sign hanging over the bar that reads:

Cigars: $10.00. Hand Job: $5.00

Checking his wallet for the necessary payment, he walks up to the bar and beckons to one of the three exceptionally attractive blondes serving drinks to an eager-looking group of men.

"Yes?" she enquires with a knowing smile, "Can I help you?"

"I was wondering, are you the one who gives the hand-jobs?"

"Yes," she purrs, "I am."

To which the man replies, "Well, wash your hands, I need a cigar."

—·—

A man went to his doctor seeking help for his terrible addiction to cigars. The doctor was quite familiar with his very compulsive patient, so he recommended an unusual and quite drastic form of aversion therapy. "When you go to bed tonight, take one of your cigars, unwrap it, and stick it completely up your asshole. Then remove it, rewrap it, and place it back with all the others in such a way that you can't tell which one it is. The aversion is obvious: you won't dare smoke any of them, not knowing which is the treated cigar."

"Thanks doc, I'll try it." And he did. But three weeks later he came back and saw the doctor again.

"What? My recommendation didn't work? It was supposed to be effective even in the most addictive of cases, such as yours is!"

"Well, it kind of worked, doc. At least I was able to transfer my addiction," said the patient.

"What in the hell is that supposed to mean?"

"Well, I don't smoke cigars anymore, but now I can't go to sleep at night unless I have a cigar shoved up my ass."

———

A defendant in a lawsuit involving large sums of money was talking to his lawyer. "If I lose this case, I'll be ruined!"

"It's in the judge's hands now," said the lawyer.

"Would it help if I sent the judge a box of cigars?"

"No! The judge is a stickler on ethical behavior. A stunt like that would prejudice him against you. He might even hold you in contempt of court."

Within the course of time, the judge rendered a decision in favor of the defendant. As the defendant left the courthouse, he said to his lawyer, "Thanks for the tip about the cigars. It really worked!"

Confidently the lawyer responded, "I'm sure we would have lost the case if you'd sent them."

"But I did send them," replied the man.

"What?" shouted the lawyer.

"That's how we won the case . . . I enclosed the plaintiff's business card."

———

Stalin, Truman, and Churchill came before St. Peter for judgment.

After passing the various tests, they were each given a request for anything they wanted.

"I want the Americans out of Russia!" cried Stalin.

"And I want the Russians destroyed," Truman retorted.

Churchill said, "I'll just have a cigar. But serve these other gentlemen first."

———

Two monks from different monasteries were old friends who shared a great fondness for cigars. Once each year when they had a chance to visit, they would pray together and, of course, light up.

Eventually, however, they became concerned that there might be some sin in their habit and they each resolved to ask their respective superiors for guidance.

When they met again, one was puffing away.

"But the head of my monastery told me it was a sin," protested the other.

"What did you ask him?" said the first.

"I asked him if it was all right to smoke during evening prayer and he said, 'No.'"

"Well," said his friend as he blew a perfect smoke ring into the air, "I asked my superior if it was all right to pray during our evening smoke and he said it was just fine!"

———

Two friends were playing golf when one pulled out a cigar. He didn't have a lighter so he asked his friend if he had one.

"I sure do," he replied and reached into his golf bag and pulled out a twelve-inch Bic lighter.

"Wow!" said his friend, "Where did you get that monster?"

"I got it from my genie."

"You have a genie?" he asked.

"Yes, he is right here in my golf bag."

"Could I see him?"

He opened his golf bag and out popped the genie.

The friend turned to the genie and said, "I am a good friend of your master. Will you grant me one wish?"

"Yes, I will," the genie said.

"I wish for a million bucks!"

The genie hopped back into the golf bag and left him standing there, waiting for his wish to be delivered.

Suddenly the sky began to darken and the sound of a million ducks flying overhead was heard.

The friend turned to his golfing partner, exclaiming, "I asked for a million bucks, not ducks!"

"I forgot to tell you the genie is hard of hearing. Do you really think I asked him for a twelve-inch Bic?"

Reasons why cigars are better than sex:

- You can *get* cigars.

- You can safely have cigars while you are driving.

- You can make cigars last as long as you want them to.

- You can have cigars even in front of your mother.

- Two people of the same sex can have cigars without being called nasty names.

- The word "commitment" doesn't scare off cigars.

- You can have cigars on top of your workbench or desk during working hours without upsetting your co-workers.

- You can ask a stranger for a cigar without getting your face slapped.

- You can have cigars at any time of the month.

- Good cigars are easy to find.

- You can have as many kinds of cigars as you can handle.

- When you have great cigars it doesn't keep your neighbors awake.

- With cigars size doesn't matter.

Chapter 10

CIGAR SMOKER HALL OF FAME

(Followed by cigar of choice, if known)

THOSE WHO HAVE GONE TO
THE GREAT CIGAR LOUNGE IN THE SKY

Red Auerbach—Hoyo De Monterrey

Milton Berle—H. Uppman

Richard Branson

George Burns—El Producto

Al Capone

Charlie Chaplin

Winston Churchill—Romeo Y Julieta. Said to smoke ten a day; has
his own size named after him.

Howard Cosell

W. C. Fields

Sigmund Freud

Che Guevara

Ernest Hemingway

Dennis Hopper

John Kennedy—Petit Upmann (Cubans). Ordered Pierre Salinger to
get him 1,000 of them before he signed the embargo that stopped
the rest of the United States from ever getting them—legally.

Mark Twain

Rudyard Kipling

Ernie Kovacs

Groucho Marx—Used the cigar as a trademark. Smoked anything he could get his hands on for as little money as possible; the cheaper the cigar, the better he liked it.

General George Patton

Babe Ruth—"Babe Ruth" Perfecto

Mark Twain—Anything he could get his hands on (except a Cuban)

John Wayne

Orson Welles

AND THOSE STILL PUFFIN' AWAY

Fidel Castro—Cohiba Corona Especial

Francis Ford Coppola

Bill Clinton—'Nuff said.

Bill Cosby—Hoyo de Monterrey double corona or an Ashton Maduro #60. Way better than "puddin' pops."

Bo Derek

Michael Douglas

Linda Evangelista

Jodie Foster

Gina Gershon

Rudy Giuliani

Gene Hackman

Lauren Hutton

Michael Jordan

Emeril Lagasse

Susan Lucci

Madonna

Bette Midler

Demi Moore

Jack Nicholson—Montecristo. I'm sure he doesn't hold 'em between
   his knees, either.

Arnold Schwarzenegger

Claudia Schiffer

Tony Soprano

Sylvester Stallone

Sharon Stone

John Travolta

Denzel Washington

Raquel Welch

Steve Wynn

Chapter 11

TOP CIGAR CITIES IN THE UNITED STATES

LAS VEGAS, NEVADA

Everyone knows that, in Nevada, anything and everything goes. Prostitution, gambling, and even smoking cigars in casinos are legal. Las Vegas is the town selected by the Retail Tobacco Dealers of America for their annual convention and trade shows. Most casinos on the Strip provide free cocktails for their gambling patrons, but some, such as Caesar's Palace, also provide free cigars. Smoking is permitted in the gaming areas of casinos, but smoking in other indoor areas within the city has been banned.

MIAMI, FLORIDA

Besides a prolific cigar culture in areas such as South Beach, where premium cigars are sold at sidewalk cafes and hotels, the section of the city known as Little Havana on Calle Ocho is deeply rooted in Cuban culture. Not only will you find great Cuban restaurants, stores, and more, but here you can find cigar stores owned by Cuban immigrants who make and sell their own brands. Although the Cuban seed tobacco may now be grown in the Dominican Republic, the handmade cigars of Little Havana are probably the closest sticks to Cuban cigars available in the United States.

Although Miami does not have its own smoking ban, the state of Florida has banned smoking in restaurants and other indoor areas in the state, but retail tobacco shops are excluded.

NEW HAVEN, CONNECTICUT

New Haven, Connecticut, has a long history of producing cigars made with Connecticut grown tobacco. The F. D. Grave factory (www.fdgrave.com) began producing cigars in New Haven in 1884. To this day, F. D. Grave still produces machine- and hand-rolled cigars with Connecticut grown tobacco.

Evermore and Farnum Drive Cigars (www.broadleafcigars.com) were acquired by National Cigar in the late 1950s. The same original New Haven cigar labels remain today and are now manufactured in Indiana with tobacco shipped from Connecticut.

The Owl Shop is the oldest tobacco shop remaining in New Haven. The original store opened in 1934. In the 1950s the shop moved from Wall Street to College Street just steps from Yale University. The Owl Shop offers an extensive selection of fine cigars and pipe tobacco. In 2006 major renovations to the shop included the addition of a full upscale bar with high-end liquor, wine, and beer. A full-service coffee bar was added in January 2008 offering fair trade coffee from around the world.

Ernest Hemingway

The Connecticut River Valley just north of Hartford, Connecticut, is the location where superior cigar wrapper leaf is grown. Just an hour from New Haven, this area still produces great tobacco for cigar makers around the world. Prior to the Cuban embargo, many outstanding Cuban cigars were rolled using Connecticut wrappers.

The Connecticut Valley Tobacconist, LLC, in the Hazardville section of Enfield, Connecticut produces private label cigars from locally grown tobacco. Cigar enthusiasts should not miss the opportunity to visit this shop and smoking lounge when in the area.

TAMPA, FLORIDA

The Tampa area is famous for cigars, and retailers such as Edwards Pipe & Tobacco and Thompson Cigar are very popular with cigar smokers. Many famous cigar makers also live in the area, as well as radio and television cigar personalities such as Cigar Dave. However, if you are looking for a taste of cigar history, Ybor City near downtown Tampa was once considered the Cigar Capital of the World (back in the late 1800s). The old cigar factories have been transformed into drinking, dining, smoking, and retail establishments, and the area is now a popular entertainment district. However, Ybor is still rich in cigar history, and the Ybor City Museum Society even has an annual Cigar Heritage Festival. There are plenty of cigar stores and establishments to choose from along 7th Avenue in Ybor City.

Although Tampa does not have its own smoking ban, the State of Florida has banned smoking in restaurants and other indoor areas in the state.

Chapter 12

THE BEST CIGAR LOUNGES, BARS, AND SHOPS IN THE UNITED STATES AND CANADA

U.S. CIGAR STORES

ALABAMA
Smoke Shop
116 Poarch Rd.
Atmore
(251) 446-8877

Little Anthony's Cigars
114 W. Magnolia Ave.
Auburn
(334) 826-7054

Tobacco Place
2941 Morgan Rd.
Bessemer
(205) 477-8008

Cahaba Spirits
3108 Cahaba Heights Rd.
Birmingham
(205) 972-0222

Cigars and More
4647 Hwy. 280 E.
Birmingham
(205) 991-3270

Cigars & More 101
1423 Gadsden Hwy.
Birmingham
(205) 655-4242

Illusions
1600 Green Springs Hwy. S.
Birmingham
(205) 326-2275

J Blackburn & Co.
3232 Galleria Circle
Birmingham
(205) 985-0409

Tobacco Leaf
253 Country Club Park
Birmingham
(205) 868-9900

Tobacco Shop
1676 Montgomery Hwy.
Birmingham
(205) 824-1644

Tobacco Station
1421 Forestdale Blvd.
Birmingham
(205) 798-9911

Smoke-N-Chew
215 N. Mulberry Ave.
Butler
(205) 459-8455

Cig & Stogie
346 Hwy. 134
Daleville
(334) 598-3056

Smokies
3669 Montgomery Hwy.
Dothan
(334) 793-5712

Tobacco Shop
2109 Ross Clark Circle
Dothan
(334) 792-3939

Tobacco Alley
525 Glover Ave.
Enterprise
(334) 347-9995

S & S Smoke Shop
542 W. Main St.
Gadsden
(256) 492-4347

Tobacco Rd.
1620 Gulf Shores Pkwy.
Gulf Shores
(251) 968-7311

Briary
609 Oak Grove Rd.
Homewood
(205) 942-9001

Amore' Pleasures
4925 University Dr. N.W.
Huntsville
(256) 837-9468

Humidor Pipe Shop Inc.
2502 Memorial Pkwy. S.W.
Huntsville
(256) 539-6431

Smokerise Tobacco
State Hwy.
Hurtsboro
(205) 590-2800

Smoke Shoppe
3802 College Ave.
Jackson
(251) 246-7401

B & K Tobacco
1205 N. Airport Rd.
Jasper
(205) 387-9166

Tobacco City 2
4544 Hwy. 14
Millbrook
(334) 285-7374

Tobacco Plus
3765 Hwy. 14
Millbrook
(334) 285-2880

Tobacco Shack
605 Alabama 3 Bay
Minette
(251) 937-3945

Tinder Box
3484 Bel Air Mall
Mobile
(251) 473-1221

Tobacco Shack
7765 Airport Blvd.
Mobile
(251) 607-9233

Tobacco Shack
5441 Hwy. 90 W. #3
Mobile
(251) 666-8116

Top Dog Tobacco
918 Alabama Ave.
Monroeville
(251) 575-2457

F & M Cigars
Minnie Brown Rd.
Montgomery
(334) 819-7955

F & M Cigars
5349 Young Barn Rd.
Montgomery
(334) 244-0061

F & M Tobacconist
Young Barn Rd.
Montgomery
(334) 244-0061

Havana Dreamin
2061 Carter Hill Rd.
Montgomery
(334) 262-3131

Randy's Tobacco Leaf
2920H Zelda Rd.
Montgomery
(334) 277-3880

Tobacco Depot
461 Eastern Blvd.
Montgomery
(334) 396-4311

Northport Smoke Shop
2110 Lurleen B Wallace Blvd.
Northport
(205) 339-5500

Tobacco Place, The
1051 Fox Run Pkwy. #102
Opelika
(334) 737-1010

Our Cigar Bar
4851 E. Entrance Wharf Pkwy.
Orange Beach
(251) 224-1687

Tobacco Rd.
25405 Perdido Beach Blvd.,
  Ste. 14
Orange Beach
(251) 981-6105

Lorillard Tobacco Co.
950 S. Memorial Dr.
Prattville
(334) 361-2840

Prattville Cigar Co.
2086 Hwy. 14 E.
Prattville
(334) 365-9181

Tobacco Co. Inc.
1730 E. Main St.
Prattville
(334) 358-9793

Tobacco Shack of Alabama
6729 Spanish Fort Blvd.
Spanish Fort
(251) 621-1122

Crimson Tobacco
1809 Skyland Blvd. E.
Tuscaloosa
(205) 507-9090

Smoke It Up Tobacco
424 15th St.
Tuscaloosa
(205) 391-4700

Smoke n Glass
1400 7th St.
Tuscaloosa
(205) 331-0878

Riverside Smoke Shop
102 River Oaks Dr.
Wetumpka
(334) 514-2700

Woodstock Tobacco
20000 Hwy. 11 #7
Woodstock
(205) 938-9099

ALASKA
Black Market
329 E. 5th Ave.
Anchorage
(907) 279-2014

Great Alaska Tobacco Co.
1650 W. Northern Lights Blvd.
Anchorage
(907) 339-0550

Great Alaska Tobacco Co.
3101 Penland Pkwy.
Anchorage
(907) 339-5250

Great Alaska Tobacco Co.
1340 Gambell St.
Anchorage
(907) 339-0250

Great Alaska Tobacco Co.
4000 W. Diamond Blvd.
Anchorage
(907) 339-1250

Great Alaska Tobacco Co.
5600 Debarr Rd.
Anchorage
(907) 339-0950

Pete's Tobacco Shop
531 E. 5th Ave.
Anchorage
(907) 274-7473

Popeye's Emporium
3231 Spenard Rd.
Anchorage
(907) 561-4434

Smoke King
4339 Mountain View Dr.
Anchorage
(907) 677-8872

Smokers Choice
3600 Minnesota Dr.
Anchorage
(907) 277-0123

Smoking Joe's
1330 Huffman Rd.
Anchorage
(907) 336-5217

Smoking Joe's
5440 E. Northern Lights Blvd.
Anchorage
(907) 337-5217

Sourdough Tobacco & Internet
735 W. 4th Ave.
Anchorage
(907) 274-6397

Tobacco Cache
601 E. Northern Lights Blvd.
Anchorage
(907) 279-9411

Great Alaska Tobacco Co.
11409 Business Blvd.
Eagle River
(907) 694-2447

Up In Smoke
12812 Old Glenn Hwy.
Eagle River
(907) 622-4545

Great Alaska Tobacco Co.
3678 College Rd.
Fairbanks
(907) 456-6530

Mr Rock & Roll
1452 S. Cushman St.
Fairbanks
(907) 458-0090

Mr Rock & Roll
2016 College Rd.
Fairbanks
(907) 455-4601

Puffin's Smoke Shop & Mini
   Store
455 3rd Ave.
Fairbanks
(907) 479-0549

Still Smoking
516 Old Steese Hwy.
Fairbanks
(907) 374-3451

Kaptain's Keg
3812 Tongass Ave.
Ketchikan
(907) 225-7363

Puffin Pipe & Tobacco Shoppe
2417 Tongass Ave.
Ketchikan
(907) 247-1768

Golden Eagle
47055 Forest Wood Ave.
Soldotna
(907) 283-0700

Great Alaskan Tobacco Co.
44224 Sterling Hwy.
Soldotna
(907) 260-7541

Hole E Smokes
43530 Kalifornsky Beach Rd.,
   Ste. 2
Soldotna
(907) 262-4838

Lucky Raven Tobacco
36312 Irons Ave.
Soldotna
(907) 260-6280

Pete's Tobacco Shop
131 George Parks Hwy.
Wasilla
(907) 357-6653

2K1 Neat Things
1150 Helen Lane
Wasilla
(907) 357-2076

Up N Smoke
951 Hermon Rd.
Wasilla
(907) 357-4545

Wild Thangz
244 Sylvan Rd.
Wasilla
(907) 357-4909

ARIZONA

Tobacco Store Xmoke City
3061 W. Apache Trail
Apache Junction
(480) 982-1390

Up in Smoke Shop 2
10262 E. Apache Trail
Apache Junction
(480) 986-6589

Ashburn Fine Cigars and
   Accessories
12725 W. Indian School Rd.
Avondale
(623) 444-2539

D J's Smoke Shop-2
70 W. Warner Rd.
Chandler
(480) 855-0838

Gila River Akimel O'Otham
   Shop
1188 S. 56th St.
Chandler
(520) 796-9931

Sam's Smoke N Stuff
411 S. Arizona Ave.
Chandler
(480) 782-7465

Oovah Smoke Shop
208 N. 16th St.
Clarkdale
(928) 634-7107

Smoke-N-Guns Fine Cigars
322 S. Main St.
Cottonwood
(928) 634-3216

Big Worms Smoke Shop
12313 Grand Ave. S.
El Mirage
(623) 583-2234

McGaughs Smoke Shop
218 S. San Francisco St.
Flagstaff
(928) 226-0100

Trader's Outlet Smoke Shop
1530 Riordan Ranch St.
Flagstaff
(928) 214-9657

Blew Smoke Premium Cigars
785 W. Warner Rd.
Gilbert
(480) 507-8800

Casa Fuma Fine Cigars
1464 E. Williamsfield Rd.,
    Ste. A105
Gilbert
(480) 794-1581

Stogie Cutter
833 N. Cooper Rd.
Gilbert
(480) 813-2628

Al Smoke Shop
15224 N. 59th Ave.
Glendale
(602) 866-2252

Smokers City
20280 N. 59th Ave.
Glendale
(623) 561-9770

Traders Smoke Shop
8110 W. Union Hills Dr.
Glendale
(623) 572-6682

Big Sticks Fine Cigars
1017 N. Dobson Rd.
Mesa
(480) 668-6099

D J's Smoke Shop-1
71840 W. Southern Ave.
Mesa
(480) 461-9174

D J's Smoke Shop-3
529 S. Gilbert Rd.
Mesa
(480) 649-8893

D J's Smoke Shop-4
7310 E. Main St.
Mesa
(480) 854-2566

D J's Smoke Shop
865 E. Isabella Ave.
Mesa
(480) 464-8598

Habanos Torres Cigar Factory
830 W. Southern Ave.
Mesa
(480) 833-0087

Smoke Shop
855 W. University Dr.
Mesa
(480) 834-3147

Sophie's Smoke Shop
1211 N. Country Club Dr.
Mesa
(480) 755-0056

Tinder Box
1457 W. Southern Ave. #110
Mesa
(480) 644-9300

Tobacco & Pipes Plus Inc.
1057 N. Mesa Dr.
Mesa
(480) 962-1699

Shades of Havana Fine Cigars
16610 N. 75th Ave.
Peoria
(623) 486-1517

Allied Tobacco
3315 W. Buckeye Rd.
Phoenix
(602) 253-0283

Bash's Smoke Shop
4247 W. Dunlap Ave.
Phoenix
(623) 915-7878

BBK Tobacco & Food Inc.
3315 W. Buckeye Rd.
Phoenix
(602) 955-3330

Blaze Tobacco & Gift
1720 W. Bell Rd.
Phoenix
(602) 993-3010

Fumar Cigars Inc.
2010 W. Parkside Lane
Phoenix
(623) 594-4020

G & S Smoke Shop
26 E. Baseline Rd.
Phoenix
(602) 276-8202

Herb 'N Legend Smoke Shop
5950 W. McDowell Rd.
Phoenix
(602) 710-1987

High Society Smoke N Stuff
9204 N. 7th St.
Phoenix
(602) 944-2774

Holy Smokes
9617 N. Metro Pkwy.
Phoenix
(602) 674-8400

It's All Goodz
12308 N. 32nd St.
Phoenix
(602) 404-7178

Just Blaze Hip Hop Smoke Shop
1740 E. McDowell Rd.
Phoenix
(602) 252-4228

Mike's Smoke Shop
8021 N. 43rd Ave.
Phoenix
(623) 435-0497

Nana's Smoke Shop
3414 W. Union Hills Dr.
Phoenix
(623) 587-0687

One Stop Smoke Shop
2113 N. 35th Ave.
Phoenix
(602) 278-3477

Popeye's Smoke Shop
3036 N. 24th St.
Phoenix
(602) 667-7763

S & M Smoke Shop
1903 W. Thunderbird Rd.
Phoenix
(602) 548-1006

7th Avenue Smoke Shop
5501 N. 7th Ave.
Phoenix
(602) 264-7516

Smokers Alley
12833 N. Cave Creek Rd.
Phoenix
(602) 923-8505

Tinder Box Ahwatukee
4611 E. Chandler Blvd. #106
Phoenix
(480) 961-7777

Tobacco & Pipes Plus Inc.
3245 E. Thomas Rd.
Phoenix
(602) 955-5077

Tobacco Giant
3411 W. Northern Ave.
Phoenix
(602) 841-9401

Ye Olde Pipe & Tobacco Shoppe
4525 N. 24th St.
Phoenix
(602) 955-7740

Yavapai Smoke Shop
1841 E. State Route 69 #101
Prescott
(928) 445-6773

Ambassador Fine Cigars
4912 E. Shea Blvd.
Scottsdale
(480) 905-1000

Cigar King
7830 E. Gelding Dr.
Scottsdale
(480) 214-0238

Coughing Canary Smoke Shop
7162 E. Thomas Rd.
Scottsdale
(480) 947-6653

Hemingway's Cigar Boutique
15211 N. Kierland Blvd.
Scottsdale
(480) 607-0777

Hiland's Cigars
6917 E. Thomas Rd.
Scottsdale
(480) 945-7050

Oggie's Cigars
13610 N. Scottsdale Rd.
Scottsdale
(480) 948-9950

Scottsdale Cigar Co.
15231 N. 87th St.
Scottsdale
(480) 991-2722

A & A Smoke
3136 S. Mill Ave.
Tempe
(480) 966-7300

Blaze
3133 S. Mill Ave.
Tempe
(480) 774-0420

Churchill's Fine Cigars
640 S. Mill Ave.
Tempe
(480) 731-5300

G & S Smoke For Less
2726 W. Southern Ave.
Tempe
(602) 438-4650

Headquarters
219 W. University Dr.
Tempe
(480) 966-6093

Hippie Gypsy
601 S. Mill Ave.
Tempe
(480) 858-0400

It's All Goodz
933 E. University Dr.
Tempe
(480) 921-7473

Sky High Smoke Shop
33 W. Southern Ave.
Tempe
(480) 557-6653

Anthony's Cigar Emporium
 East
4811 E. Grant Rd.
Tucson
(520) 324-0303

Head East Smoke Shop
8739 E. Broadway Blvd.
Tucson
(520) 886-0393

Hippie Gypsy
351 N. 4th Ave.
Tucson
(520) 624-0667

Moon Smoke Shop
120 W. Grant Rd.
Tucson
(520) 622-7261

Moon Smoke Shop
7151 E. Broadway Blvd.
Tucson
(520) 885-1457

Tinder Box
5350 E. Broadway Blvd.
Tucson
(520) 747-4807

Tobacco Barn
7310 S. Nogales Hwy.
Tucson
(520) 889-9591

ARKANSAS

Tobacco Town
903 N. Church St.
Atkins
(479) 641-1087

Alford Tobacco Inc.
1400 W. Dewitt Henry Dr. #Bb
Beebe
(501) 882-3321

Tobacco Rack Inc.
810 Edison Ave.
Benton
(501) 315-1224

Tobacco Rack Inc.
1218 Military Rd.
Benton
(501) 315-6627

Tobacco Shack
1800 N. Reynolds Rd.
Bryant
(501) 847-6656

Alford Tobacco Store
521 W. Main St.
Cabot
(501) 941-3179

Ward Tobacco Store
613 Hickory Lane
Cabot
(501) 843-1076

Walker Tobacco Shop
503 Madison St.
Clarendon
(870) 747-5905

Tobacco World
296 Main St.
Clinton
(501) 745-7680

Tobacco Depot
505 E. Dave Ward Dr. #5
Conway
(501) 764-0271

Tobacco Station USA
2665 Donaghey Ave.
Conway
(501) 450-9985

White River Tobacco Co.
99 Spring St.
Eureka Springs
(479) 253-5350

Taylors Pipe & Tobacco Shop
5304 Rogers Ave.
Fort Smith
(479) 452-1449

Greenbrier Discount Tobacco
8 S. Broadview St.
Greenbrier
(501) 679-7187

Tobacco World
8155 Edgemont Rd.
Greers Ferry
(501) 825-8256

Tobacco Station USA
1104 N. Illinois Ave.
Harrisburg
(870) 578-2462

Heber Springs Discount
   Tobacco
2210 State Hwy. 25 Spur
Heber Springs
(501) 362-6288

Churchill's Fine Cigars
801 Central Ave.
Hot Springs
(501) 623-2866

Cigar World Inc.
3145 Central Ave.
Hot Springs
(501) 624-0868

Tobacco Junction
1545 Malvern Ave.
Hot Springs
(501) 321-2111

Tobacco Town
649 E. Grand Ave.
Hot Springs
(501) 623-2355

Tobacco World
14509A Hwy. 107
Jacksonville
(501) 833-8433

K J Tobacco Store
348 Cw Rd.
Judsonia
(501) 729-1010

Linda's Tobacco World
1403 John Barrow Rd.
Little Rock
(501) 221-3813

Lorillard Tobacco Co.
1200 John Barrow Rd.
Little Rock
(501) 228-7660

Smoke Break
207 W. Capitol Ave.
Little Rock
(501) 374-7833

Tobacco Road
6801 W. 12th St.
Little Rock
(501) 907-6006

Tobacco World of Mayflower
620 Hwy. 365
Mayflower
(501) 470-0149

Smoke Shop
1211 Hwy. 9
Morrilton
(501) 354-9177

Tobacco Corner Plus
319 E. Broadway St.
Morrilton
(501) 977-1312

Tobacco Town
1512 E. Harding St.
Morrilton
(501) 208-5641

Tobacco Station USA
203 US 62
Mountain Home
(870) 425-2701

Tobacco Rack Inc.
4434 Camp Robinson Rd.
North Little Rock
(501) 753-1312

Tobacco Rack Inc.
4321 E. Broadway St.
North Little Rock
(501) 945-2949

Fourche Valley Tobacco
115 N. Magnolia St.
Perryville
(501) 889-2268

D & H Tobacco Store
2501 S. Bay St.
Pine Bluff
(870) 535-8008

Tobacco World
29 College St. E.
Quitman
(501) 589-3533

Davis' Pipe & Tobacco Shop
1509 E. Main St. #B
Russellville
(479) 968-6760

Tobacco Row
200 E. 4th St.
Russellville
(479) 967-6431

Holy Smokes Tobacco Shop
811 S. Main St.
Searcy
(501) 368-0908

Tobacco Station USA
2909 E. Race Ave.
Searcy
(501) 268-7789

Shirley Tobacco Shop
9667 Hwy. 16 E.
Shirley
(501) 723-8303

M & L Tobacco Store
706 Hwy. 67 S.
Tuckerman
(870) 349-2343

CALIFORNIA
Paradise Cigar
2012 S. Flippen Dr.
Anaheim
(714) 539-2575

Smoke Signals
15 S. Main St.
Angels Camp
(209) 736-9500

Belmont Smoke Shop &
   Novelties
840 El Camino Real
Belmont
(650) 508-1805

Whelan's Cigar Store
2486 Bancroft Way
Berkeley
(510) 549-3218

Buena Vista Cigar Club
9715 Santa Monica Blvd.
Beverly Hills
(310) 273-8100

Kramer's Pipe & Tobacco Shop
9531 Santa Monica Blvd.
Beverly Hills
(310) 273-9777

Harry's Tobacco Shop
2309 W. Olive Ave.
Burbank
(818) 566-4260

Burlingame Smoke Shop
1400 Burlingame Ave.
Burlingame
(650) 343-3363

Campbell Cigars
831 Union Ave.
Campbell
(408) 371-3099

Twisted
7777 Sunrise Blvd.
Citrus Heights
(916) 729-4141

Cigars Limited
630 Clovis Ave.
Clovis
(559) 297-0312

One World Smoke Shop
2075 Newport Blvd.
Costa Mesa
(949) 548-4030

Up n Smoke
2750 Harbor Blvd.
Costa Mesa
(714) 557-4664

Nirvana Smoke & Gift Shop
10800 Washington Blvd.
Culver City
(310) 559-9420

Rockys Smoke Shop
39471 Fremont Blvd.
Fremont
(510) 252-9233

Wonderland Smoke Shop
40900 Fremont Blvd.
Fremont
(510) 226-9900

Cigar Mas Fino
1568 E. Nees Ave.
Fresno
(559) 322-8080

Club Habanos Inc
6759 N. Palm Ave.
Fresno
(559) 449-2447

Kaleidoscope Tobacco & Gifts
4565 N. Blackstone Ave.
Fresno
(559) 229-5683

Perfect Blend Fine Cigars
729 E. Olive Ave.
Fresno
(559) 486-0400

Smoke Shop
3034 W. Bullard Ave.
Fresno
(559) 432-3047

Stuffed Pipe
2377 E. Shaw Ave.
Fresno
(559) 225-4622

Vino 100–Fresno
NE Corner of Ceder & Shepherd
528 E. Champlain Dr. #108
Fresno
(559) 434-1771

Red Cloud Fine Cigars Tobacco
118 W. Wilshire Ave.
Fullerton
(714) 680-6200

Stardust Smoke Shop
1330A E. Chapman Ave.
Fullerton
(714) 871-8105

Brand Cigar Club
154 S. Brand Blvd.
Glendale
(818) 551-5553

Planet Tobacco
1243 W. Glenoaks Blvd.
Glendale
(818) 500-7445

Smoke N' Sticks
11027 Balboa Blvd.
Granada Hills
(818) 363-0021

Bay Book & Tobacco Co.
80 Cabrillo Hwy. N.
Halfmoon Bay
(650) 726-3488

Glass Garden Smoke Shop
   and Gifts
17841 Beach Blvd.
Huntington Beach
(714) 848-7179

Hoffer's Cigar Bar
8282 La Mesa Blvd.
La Mesa
(619) 466-8282

AA Tobacco Barn Pipe Shop
23532 El Toro Rd.
Lake Forest
(949) 830-7110

Aficionado Cigar Diamond
   Crown Lounge
23825 El Toro Rd.
Lake Forest
(949) 829-8474

A1 Smoke & Cigar
22359 El Toro Rd.
Lake Forest
(949) 707-0638

Charlotte's Web
2160 Railroad Ave.
Livermore
(925) 449-6165

Bo's Cigar Lounge
4501 E. Carson St.
Long Beach
(562) 429-5600

Cigar Lounge
202 Nieto Ave.
Long Beach
(562) 439-8284

Cohiba Cigars
110 E. Broadway
Long Beach
(562) 491-5220

Exhale Cafe
674 Redondo Ave.
Long Beach
(562) 434-6799

Heads Up Smoke Shop
1742 E. Broadway
Long Beach
(562) 432-9600

Taylors Tobacco House
5937 E. Spring St.
Long Beach
(562) 377-0700

Tobacco Republic Inc
3589 Taylor Rd.
Loomis
(916) 652-2010

Edward's Pipe & Tobacco
4546 El Camino Real
Los Altos
(650) 948-7473

Diplomat Cigar Shop
806 W. 7th St.
Los Angeles
(213) 627-6434

Hollywood Smoke Shop
6423 Hollywood Blvd.
Los Angeles
(323) 464-2765

Melrose Smoke Shop
7801 Melrose Ave.
Los Angeles
(323) 655-6600

Mike's Smoke Shop
6624 Hollywood Blvd.
Los Angeles
(323) 461-8508

2nd Street Cigar & Gallery
124 W. 2nd St.
Los Angeles
(213) 452-4427

Tabu Smoke Shop
6315 Hollywood Blvd.
Los Angeles
(323) 462-2125

Tobacco Cheaper Store
11221 National Blvd.
Los Angeles
(310) 479-8379

VIP Smoke Shop
7131 W. Sunset Blvd.
Los Angeles
(323) 969-8233

Wally's Wine & Spirits
2107 Westwood Blvd.
Los Angeles
(310) 475-0606

V Cut Smoke Shop
8172 Melrose Ave.
Los Angeles
(323) 655-5959

Old Knickerbockers
  Tobacconist
555 Santa Cruz Ave.
Menlo Park
(650) 327-7473

Cigar Monkey
1716 Canal St.
Merced
(209) 384-7473

Jim Mate Pipe & Tobacco Shop
355 Marin Ave.
Mill Valley
(415) 388-8964

Telford's Pipe Shop
664 Redwood Hwy.,
  Frontage Rd.
Mill Valley
(415) 388-0440

Cheroot Lounge
915 10th St.
Modesto
(209) 492-9141

No Limit Smoke Shop
1209 McHenry Ave.
Modesto
(209) 576-1699

Still Smoking
1313 J St.
Modesto
(209) 574-0681

Cool Cat Cigars
625 Cannery Row
Monterey
(831) 643-2665

Hellam's Tobacco Shop
423 Alvarado St.
Monterey
(831) 373-2816

Morgan Hill Tobacco Co.
17430 Monterey Rd.
Morgan Hill
(408) 776-7667

Fatty Zone
1398 W. El Camino Real
Mountain View
(650) 965-0313

Baker Street Downtown
1018 1st St.
Napa
(707) 255-4434

Doc of Rock
1811 Old Sonoma Rd.
Napa
(707) 226-7652

Newport Tobacco
997 Newport Center Dr.
Newport Beach
(949) 644-5153

Dementia
6334 Laurel Canyon Blvd.
North Hollywood
(818) 506-3011

Divine Smoke Shop
5056 Lankershim Blvd.
North Hollywood
(818) 508-9948

Vendome Wine & Spirits
10600 Riverside Dr.
North Hollywood
(818) 766-9593

Holy Smoke Cigar Shop
9072 Tampa Ave.
Northridge
(818) 407-0114

Piedmont Tobacconist
17 Glen Ave.
Oakland
(510) 652-7473

Puff 'N Stuff Smoke Shop
4051 Foothill Blvd.
Oakland
(510) 533-3161

Cigar Grotto
220 N. Coast Hwy.
Oceanside
(760) 722-1602

Smoke Shop
3809 Plaza Dr.
Oceanside
(760) 941-3746

Cohiba Cigar Lounge
20 City Blvd. W.
Orange
(714) 769-3769

Wine Exchange
1500 E. Village Way # 2368
Orange
(714) 974-1454

Native Made Tobacco Shop
559 S. Palm Canyon Dr.
Palm Springs
(760) 318-6555

Mac's Smoke Shop Inc.
534 Emerson St.
Palo Alto
(650) 323-3724

Ceniza Cigar Lounge
260 E. Colorado Blvd.
Pasadena
(626) 795-4664

Cigars By Chivas
58 S. De Lacey Ave.
Pasadena
(626) 395-7475

Le Petit Vendome
906 Granite Dr.
Pasadena
(626) 396-9234

Puffs Smoke Shop
9458 Whittier Blvd.
Pico Rivera
(562) 949-4222

Legends Smoke Shop
565 Contra Costa Blvd.
Pleasant Hill
(925) 691-5006

The Humidor Cigars and Gifts
12 E. Vine St.
Redlands
(909) 792-4393

Stogies Smoke Shop
3288 Pierce St.
Richmond
(510) 558-1510

Mission Tobacco Lounge
3630 University Ave.
Riverside
(951) 682-4427

Huckleberry's
627 Silver Spur Rd.
Rolling Hills Estates
(310) 265-2489

Ken's Smoke Shop
1431 W. Rosamond Blvd.
Rosamond
(661) 256-6830

Millenium Smoke Shop
1000 Melody Lane
Roseville
(916) 772-6969

Blow and Tell Smoke Shop
1914 Fulton Ave.
Sacramento
(916) 486-2569

Briar Patch
2529 Fair Oaks Blvd.
Sacramento
(916) 929-8965

J R Smoke Shop
5555 Sky Pkwy.
Sacramento
(916) 395-1577

Rodney's Cigar & Liquor Store
1000 J St.
Sacramento
(916) 442-5998

Sunshine Smoke Shop
4501 Auburn Blvd.
Sacramento
(916) 972-0513

Tobacco Road
2912 Pasatiempo Place
Sacramento
(916) 489-4590

Tower Pipes & Cigars
2518 Land Park Dr.
Sacramento
(916) 443-8466

Wild Zone
8710 La Riviera Dr.
Sacramento
(916) 362-0108

Ludwig's Fine Wine, Liquor &
   Smoke Shop
431 San Anselmo Ave.
San Anselmo
(415) 456-1820

40th Smoke Shop
267 E. 40th St.
San Bernardino
(909) 881-6187

Cigars & More
666 Laurel St.
San Carlos
(650) 596-9752

Black
5017 Newport Ave.
San Diego
(619) 222-5498

Churchill Cigar Lounge
2415 San Diego Ave.
San Diego
(619) 546-7758

Crossroads Smoke Shop
972 Garnet Ave.
San Diego
(858) 272-3015

Cuban Cigar Factory
551 5th Ave.
San Diego
(619) 238-2496

Excalibur Cigar & Wine Bar
7094 Miramar Rd.
San Diego
(858) 549-4422

Old Town
2733 San Diego Ave.
San Diego
(619) 291-7833

Racine and Laramie Ltd.
2737 San Diego Ave.
San Diego
(619) 291-7833

California Tobacco Center
1501 Polk St.
San Francisco
(415)885-5479

Castro Smoke House
409 Castro St.
San Francisco
(415) 552-7411

Geary Street Smoke Shop
599 Geary St.
San Francisco
(415) 673-0154

Good Fellows
473 Haight St.
San Francisco
(415) 255-1323

Grant's Tobacconists
562 Market St.
San Francisco
(415) 981-1000

Haight Street Tobacco
1827 Haight St.
San Francisco
(415) 221-3415

Humidor
275 Battery St.
San Francisco
(415) 362-1405

Mimi's Smoke Shop
581 Ellis St.
San Francisco
(415) 771-5111

Mission Smoke Shop
2059 Mission St.
San Francisco
(415) 252-1250

Puff Puff Pass
1467 Haight St.
San Francisco
(415) 558-9593

Stogies Inc.
2801 Jones St.
San Francisco
(415) 771-7767

Store on The Corner
121 New Montgomery St.
San Francisco
(415) 781-3348

Blunts Tobacco
1814 Hillsdale Ave.
San Jose
(408) 269-3832

Club Havana Premium Cigars
860 El Paseo de Saratoga
San Jose
(408) 871-2199

Giza
18 N. 1st St.
San Jose
(408) 998-4622

McKee Smoke Shop
311 N. Capitol Ave.
San Jose
(408) 926-1791

Smoker's Paradise
3623 Union Ave.
San Jose
(408) 377-1335

West Coast Cigars
1650 Almaden Rd.
San Jose
(408) 283-9323

Cloud 9 Smoke Shop & Hookah
Lounge
584 California Blvd.
San Luis Obispo
(805) 593-0420

Sanctuary Tobacco Shop
1111 Chorro St.
San Luis Obispo
(805) 543-1958

Sub, The
295 Higuera St.
San Luis Obispo
(805) 541-3735

Cigar Loft
106 W. 25th Ave.
San Mateo
(650) 312-1141

Tobacco Leaf
2470 S. Western Ave.
San Pedro
(424) 772-6400

J's Paradise 2
413 W. 17th St.
Santa Ana
(714) 541-0996

Yogi's Smoke Shop
2114 N. Tustin Ave.
Santa Ana
(714) 541-1605

Santa Barbara Cigar &
Tobacco
10 W. Figueroa St.
Santa Barbara
(805) 963-1979

Pipe Line
818 Pacific Ave.
Santa Cruz
(831) 425-7473

Lone Wolf Fine Cigars & Men's
Accessories
223B Broadway
Santa Monica
(310) 458-5441

Homeblown Glass
705 4th St.
Santa Rosa
(707) 591-0420

Mighty Quinn
3372 Santa Rosa Ave.
Santa Rosa
(707) 545-4975

Peacepipe Smoke Shop
622 Santa Rosa Ave.
Santa Rosa
(707) 541-7016

Daddy's Pipes & Smoking
Access
14430 Ventura Blvd.
Sherman Oaks
(818) 817-9517

Sportsman
90 S. Washington St.
Sonora
(209) 532-1716

Fair Oaks Cigars
806 Fair Oaks Ave.
South Pasadena
(626) 441-1457

Core-Mark International Inc.
Ste. 415, 395 Oyster Point Blvd.
South San Francisco
(650) 873-2673

Smoke Zone
25886 The Old Rd.
Stevenson Ranch
(661) 284-1298

Tobacco Leaf Tobacconist
209 Lincoln Center
Stockton
(209) 474-8216

Hyphy Smoke Shop
8626 N. Lower Sacramento Rd.
Stocton
(209) 951-1340

Big Easy
12604 Ventura Blvd.
Studio City
(818) 762-3279

Murphy Street Smoke Shop
114 S. Murphy Ave.
Sunnyvale
(408) 735-9127

Zarka Cigar Lounge & Bar
28120 Jefferson Ave.
Temecula
(951) 587-9854

Old Oaks Cigar Co.
3006 E. Thousand Oaks Blvd.
Thousand Oaks
(805) 494-1886

Tobacco Hut
658 Thousand Oaks Blvd.
Thousand Oaks
(805) 777-1001

Casillas Cigars
333 Merchant St.
Vacaville
(707) 448-8355

Green House Smoke Shop
1428 Abbot Kinney Blvd.
Venice
(310) 450-6420

Pipeline Smoke Shop
228 E. Thompson Blvd.
Ventura
(805) 643-4420

Wild Side Smoke Shop
2850 Johnson Dr.
Ventura
(805) 644-4060

Visalia Mall: Regis Salon
2031 S. Mooney Blvd.
Visalia
(559) 625-5800

Tinder Box
8621 Santa Monica Blvd.
West Hollywood
(310) 659-6464

Havana House Cigars
7020 Greenleaf Ave.
Whittier
(562) 698-2245

COLORADO
Smoker Friendly
9588 W. 58th Ave.
Arvada
(303) 425-6988

Smokers Delight
2295 S. Chambers Rd.
Aurora
(303) 337-6242

Bova's Pantry
1325 Broadway St.
Boulder
(303) 449-0874

Mile High Pipes & Tobacco
1144 Pearl St.
Boulder
(303) 443-7473

Smoker Friendly
6650 W. 120th Ave.
Broomfield
(303) 635-0608

Old West Cigar & Tobacco Co.
229 E. Pikes Peak Ave.
Colorado Springs
(719) 635-0211

Peak Cigars & Pipes
410 S. 8th St.
Colorado Springs
(719) 477-1010

Smoker King
1951 W. Uintah St.
Colorado Springs
(719) 633-6320

Stag Tobacconist
4109 Austin Bluffs Pkwy.
Colorado Springs
(719) 633-0669

Cigar & Tobacco World
5227 Leetsdale Dr.
Denver
(303) 321-7308

Cigars on 6th
707 E. 6th Ave.
Denver
(303) 830-8100

El Cid's Ltd.
4401 Zenobia St.
Denver
(303) 477-2864

Havana's Fine Cigars
2727 E. 2nd Ave.
Denver
(303) 355-2003

Head Quarters Gift Shop
1301 Marion St.
Denver
(303) 830-2444

Heads of State
3015 W. 44th Ave.
Denver
(303) 433-6585

Herbal Daze
4530 E. Colfax Ave.
Denver
(303) 333-1445

Jerri's Tobacco Shop & Fine
Wines
500 16th St.
Denver
(303) 825-3522

Palma Cigar Co.
2207 Larimer St.
Denver
(303) 297-3244

Prince Philip's Pipes
& Tobacco
3333 S. Tamarac Dr.
Denver
(303) 695-1959

Purple Haze
1951 S. Broadway
Denver
(303) 715-0055

Purple Haze
2017 E. Colfax Ave.
Denver
(303) 329-0055

Smokey's Pipe & Tobacco
10019 E. Hampden Ave.
Denver
(303) 695-9747

Tewksbury & Co.
1512 Larimer St.
Denver
(303) 825-1880

What's Knot to Love
919 E. Colfax Ave.
Denver
(303) 832-2440

Durango Smoke Shop
113 W. College Dr.
Durango
(970) 247-9115

Dementia
4356 S. Broadway
Englewood
(303) 781-1205

Edward's Pipe & Tobacco
Shop
3439 S. Broadway
Englewood
(303) 781-7662

Stanley Pappas Cigar
9600 E. Arapahoe Rd.
Englewood
(303) 792-2519

Tobacco Corner
201 E. Main St.
Florence
(719) 784-2314

Edward's Pipe & Tobacco
111 E. Prospect Rd.
Fort Collins
(970) 226-5311

Lazy J's Smoke Shop
1700 S. College Ave.
Fort Collins
(970) 282-4467

Istanbul
630 26th St.
Greeley
(970) 353-3994

Barlow's Premium Cigars &
Pipe
2770 Arapahoe Rd.
Lafayette
(303) 926-1002

Stone Face Smoke Shop
105 N. Public Rd.
Lafayette
(303) 926-4108

Freedom Pipe & Tobacco
1695 Wadsworth Blvd.
Lakewood
(303) 238-3736

Heads of State
9715 W. Colfax Ave.
Lakewood
(303) 202-9400

Lazy J's
10672 W. Alameda Ave.
Lakewood
(303) 985-2113

Tobacco Leaf
7111 W. Alameda Ave.
Lakewood
(303) 274-8720

Rocky Mountain Pipeline
11716 W. Colfax Ave.
Lakewood
(303) 233-7473

Gars & Grapes
9046 W. Bowles Ave.
Littleton
(303) 904-7650

Nickle Cigar
6679 W. Ken Caryl Ave.
Littleton
(303) 904-8760

Stogies & Bogeys USA
9535 Park Meadows Dr.
Lone Tree
(303) 790-0900

Havana Manor Cigars and
Pipes
W. Dillon Rd.
Louisville
(303) 666-6134

Tobacco Haven
10663 Melody Dr.
Northglenn
(303) 450-0953

All Puffed Out Pipe
& Tobacco
9071 Washington St.
Thornton
(303) 227-6796

Get Hi Gallery
41184 US 6
Vail
(970) 748-9995

Mile High Pipes & Tobacco
3001 W. 74th Ave.
Westminster
(303) 426-6343

Original Cigar Store
8715 N. Sheridan Blvd.
Westminster
(303) 430-7446

World Class Cigars
4800 Wadsworth Blvd.
Wheat Ridge
(303) 403-9000

CONNECTICUT

Cigar World
126 Mill St.
Berlin
(860) 828-7870

Bethel Smoke Shop
18 P T Barnum Square
Bethel
(203) 748-6974

Branford Cigar Co
635 W. Main St.
Branford
(203) 488-8550

Tony's Smoke Shop Outlet
2738 Main St.
Bridgeport
(203) 367-8558

Royale Tobacco
235 Federal Rd.
Brookfield
(203) 775-6325

Up In Smoke
136 Berlin Rd.
Cromwell
(860) 632-1962

Butthead's Tobacco
Emporium
45 Padanaram Rd.
Danbury
(203) 792-4327

Street Corner News
7 Backus Ave.
Danbury
(203) 790-9595

N & S Smoke Junction
54 Pershing Dr.
Derby
(203) 735-3010

United Cigar LLC
41 Elizabeth St.
Derby
(203) 734-2435

Smoke-N-Leather
348 Hazard Ave.
Enfield
(860) 749-9614

Arcade Cigars
2060 Post Rd.
Fairfield
(203) 259-1994

Best Cigar Co.
2 Canal Path
Farmington
(860) 677-2866

Byram Smoke Shop Inc.
111 Mill St.
Greenwich
(203) 531-2751

Whitfield Tobacco
1300 Boston Post Rd.
Guilford
(203) 453-4029

Smoker's Discount World
1394 Dixwell Ave.
Hamden
(203) 248-6099

Tobacco Shop LLC
55 Asylum St.
Hartford
(860) 524-8577

Carolina Tobacco Emporium
406 Middle Turnpike W.
Manchester
(860) 649-0090

Tobacco World
626 E. Main St.
Meriden
(203) 235-2558

Tobacco Junction LLC
759 Boston Post Rd.
Milford
(203) 877-4069

Monroe Smoke Shop
181 Main St.
Monroe
(203) 445-9994

Smoke Land
727 Rubber Ave.
Naugatuck
(203) 720-2163

Stogies Cigar & Tobacco Shop
100 Church St.
Naugatuck
(203) 729-3031

Jimmy's Quality Smoke Shop
64 W. Main St.
New Britain
(860) 229-2074

Cigarero Cigar Shop
16 Fountain St.
New Haven
(203) 387-4995

Owl Shop LLC
268 College St.
New Haven
(203) 624-3250

Archway News
64 Bank St.
New Milford
(860) 355-1557

Butthead's Tobacco Emporium
71 S. Main St.
Newtown
(203) 364-0300

Newtown Convenience
22 Church Hill Rd.
Newtown
(203) 270-3428

Cigar Factory Outlet
27 Hanford Place
Norwalk
(203) 854-9594

Smoker's Paradise
311 Main St.
Plymouth
(860) 314-8022

Prospect Smoke Shop
50 Waterbury Rd.
Prospect
(203) 758-0170

Joe's Cigar Shop
781 Cromwell Ave.
Rocky Hill
(860) 257-8504

Torpedoes Smoke Shop
922 Hopmeadow St.
Simsbury
(860) 658-7502

Grand Prix Cigars LLC
1455 Southford Rd.
Southbury
(203) 262-4427

Smoke Shop, The
77 Main St. N.
Southbury
(203) 264-5075

Wallingford Smoke
   Shop LLC
682 Queen St.
Southington
(860) 621-9296

Esquire Cigars LLC
871 Barnum Ave. Cutoff
Stratford
(203) 380-9771

S A Cigar Junction LLC
1030 Barnum Ave. # 2
Stratford
(203) 378-1600

Laraia's Tobacco Store
41 Main St.
Torrington
(860) 489-9864

Wallingford Tobacco
950 Yale Ave.
Wallingford
(203) 265-6099

Tobacco Plus LLC
515 Wolcott St.
Waterbury
(203) 573-0036

DELAWARE
Tobacco Café
1839 Pulaski Hwy.
Bear
(302) 836-0300

Ridge Tobacco
311 Ridge Rd.
Claymont
(302) 792-8390

Joe's Tobacco Super Store
38627 Benro Dr. # 2
Delmar
(302) 846-2898

Airport News Inc.
203 N. Dupont Hwy.
New Castle
(302) 325-1664

Butts & Bets
103 E. Hazeldell Ave.
New Castle
(302) 655-6002

Books & News Plus
756 E. Chestnut Hill Rd.
Newark
(302) 366-0102

Frolic On Main Street
170 E. Main St., Second Floor
Newark
(302) 283-1300

General Tobacco Inc.
250 Corporate Blvd.
Newark
(302) 737-5565

Old Baltimore Pike Cigarettes
786 Old Baltimore Pike
Newark
(302) 455-1099

Back Bay Tobacco
3 Back Bay
Rehoboth Beach
(302) 947-1199

Cigar World
18701 Coastal Hwy. # 10
Rehoboth Beach
(302) 644-3113

Rehoboth Tobacco & Gifts
4 N. 1st St.
Rehoboth Beach
(302) 226-5280

Payless Tobacco
1024 W. Stein Hwy.
Seaford
(302) 628-4343

Books and Tobacco Inc.
4555 Kirkwood Hwy.
Wilmington
(302) 994-3156

C & D Smoke Shop
333 New Castle Ave.
Wilmington
(302) 654-0010

Lee's Smoke Shop
718 N. Market St.
Wilmington
(302) 778-2177

Tobacco Field
5621 Concord Pike
Wilmington
(302) 477-1124

Tobacco Village
4011 Concord Pike
Wilmington
(302) 478-5075

DISTRICT OF COLUMBIA

Capital Hill Premium Cigars
1006 Florida Ave. N.E.
Washington
(202) 396-8006

Cigar Bar Butlers
1000 H St. N.W.
Washington
(202) 637-4765

Georgetown Tobacco
3144 M St. N.W.
Washington
(202) 338-5100

Grand Havana Room House
of Cigars
1220 19th St. N.W.
Washington
(202) 955-4575

Havana Max
3249 M St. N.W.
Washington
(202) 337-8897

J R Cigars
1730 L St. N.W.
Washington
(202) 296-3872

President Cigars
4936 Wisconsin Ave. N.W.
Washington
(202) 237-5172

President Cigars
50 Massachusetts Ave N.E.
#tt009
Washington
(202) 289-3778

President Cigars
Union Station
Washington
(202) 289-2559

Shelly's Backroom
1331 F St. N.W.
Washington
(202) 737-3003

Smokey's
4714 14th St. N.W.
Washington
(202) 723-8960

TG Cigar
1118 9th St. N.W.
Washington
(202) 289-8684

W Curtis Draper Inc.
640 14th St. N.W.
Washington
(202) 638-2555

FLORIDA
Mike's Cigars
1030 Kane Concourse
Bay Harbor Isles
(305) 866-2277

Bennington Tobacconist of
   Boca
501 S.E. Mizner Blvd.
Boca Raton
(561) 391-1372

Greatful J's Too Inc.
2401 N. Federal Hwy.
Boca Raton
(561) 362-6100

Cape Smoke Shop
3512 Del Prado Blvd. S.
Cape Coral
(239) 549-8809

Cigar Central
521 Chestnut St.
Clearwater
(727) 298-8848

Erik's Smoke Shop
714 S. Ft. Harrison Ave.
Clearwater
(727) 330-7890

Shop 2420
2420 Gulf to Bay Blvd.
Clearwater
(727) 712-8676

Olde Colonial Havana Cigar
   Co.
625 Brevard Ave.
Cocoa
(321) 636-0202

Cigars & Expresso
9623 W. Sample Rd.
Coral Springs
(954) 255-5280

Reel Smokers Cigar
504 S. Federal Hwy.
Deerfield Beach
(954) 429-1335

Carolina Cigar Co.
630 E. Atlantic Ave.
Delray Beach
(561) 330-6683

Florida Cigar Co.
1527 N. Federal Hwy.
Fort Lauderdale
(954) 563-4677

Nick's Cigar Co.
5150 N.W. 167th St.
Hialeah
(305) 266-9907

Cuenca Cigars Shop
1928 Harrison St., Ste. B
Hollywood
(866) 417-9454

Island Smoke Shop
103400 Overseas Hwy.
Key Largo
(305) 453-4014

Ol' Times Cigars & Lounge
10401 US 441
Leesburg
(352) 787-2450

Executive Cigar Shop
   & Lounge
837 E. New Haven Ave.
Melbourne
(321) 733-4554

Casa Felipe Miami
900 S.W. 8th St.
Miami
(305) 860-3230

El Titan De Bronze Cigar
   Manufacturing
1071 S.W. 8th St.
Miami
(305) 860-1412

High Tide Inc.
9814 S. Dixie Hwy.
Miami
(305) 670-6633

Inter-America Cigar Co.
1876 N.W. 21st Terrace
Miami
(305) 547-2151

Public House
1059 Collins Ave.
Miami Beach
(305) 532-9772

Havana Cigar Club
15458 N.W. 77th Court
Miami Lakes
(305) 825-5827

Heavenly Cigar Co.
2154 Trade Center Way
Naples
(239) 262-7250

Dosal Tobacco
4775 N.W. 132nd St.
Opa Locka
(305) 685-2949

Maduros Cigar and Wine Bar
3593 S. Orange Ave.
Orlando
(407) 857-4414

Medici Cigars
15 Alafaya Woods Blvd.
Oviedo
(407) 365-8333

House of Fun
36279 US Hwy. 19 N.
Palm Harbor
(727) 784-9820

Havana House
Plantation Promenade Shops
10047 Cleary Blvd.
Plantation
(954) 474-9799

Cigar Loft
2448 Central Ave.
St. Petersburg
(727) 388-6992

Central Cigars
273 Central Ave.
St. Petersburg
(727) 898-2442

Latin Quarter House of Cigars
7400 Gulf Blvd.
St. Petersburg Beach
(727) 393-4000

Bab Al Hara Hookah Lounge
10710 N. 56th St.
Tampa
(813) 985-4120

Havana Dream Cigar Factory
1600 E. 8th Ave.
Tampa
(813) 241-4010

House of Delmage
405 S. 22nd St.
Tampa
(813) 248-5776

King Corona Cigars Cafe
and Bar
1523 E. 7th Ave.
Tampa
(813) 241-9109

Thompson Group Inc.
5401 Hangar Court
Tampa
(813) 884-6344

Smoke Inn
801 Village Blvd.
West Palm Beach
(561) 721-2383

GEORGIA

Forty Two Degrees Athens
253 W. Washington St.
Athens
(706) 353-4202

Ash Cigar Co. LLC
2571 Piedmont Rd. N.E.
Atlanta
(404) 816-4406

Buckhead Cigar Club LLC
3400 Around Lenox Rd. N.E.
Atlanta
(404) 844-0400

Edwards Pipe and Cigar
3137 Piedmont Rd. N.E.
Atlanta
(404) 233-8082

Highland Tobacco & Gifts
1002 Virginia Ave. N.E.
Atlanta
(404) 817-0470

J's Cigars & Coffee House
2072 Defoors Ferry Rd. N.W.
Atlanta
(404) 355-2342

Stuff Your Own.Com
5930 Branden Hill Lane
Buford
(770) 932-9436

Blown Away Tobacco & Smoke
   Shop
1410 Klondike Rd.
Conyers
(678) 413-0203

A K Tobacco & Gift Shop
2515 Cleveland Hwy.
Dalton
(706) 428-0703

Puff 'N' Stuff
2523 Lawrenceville Hwy.
Decatur
(770) 908-9388

Chief's Cigar, The
Alpine Village Shoppes
8160 S. Main St.
Helen
(706) 878-7788

Modern Age Tobacco Shop
4121 Peach Orchard Rd.
Hephzibah
(706) 592-6283

Tobacco House
5900 Sugarloaf Pkwy.
Lawrenceville
(678) 847-0042

Savannah Cigars Inc
308 W. Congress St.
Savannah
(912) 233-2643

Verderys Lamps Midtown
280 Eisenhower Dr.
Savannah
(912) 691-0807

PD Cigar
5531 N. Henry Blvd.
Stockbridge
(678) 565-8151

Smokers Paradise
4090 Johns Creek Pkwy.
Suwanee
(770) 814-2155

HAWAII
Pipeline Smoke Shop
1019 University Ave.
Honolulu
(808) 942-4700

Sam's Club
750 Keeaumoku St.
Honolulu
(808) 945-9841

Smokey's
159 Kaiulani Ave.
Honolulu
(808) 926-9099

Sir Wilfred's
1221 Honoapiilani Hwy.
Lahaina
(808) 667-1941

IDAHO
Big Smoke
2127 Broadway Ave.
Boise
(208) 345-3043

Big Smoke
10658 W. Overland Rd.
Boise
(208) 377-1050

Big Smoke
3826 W. State St.
Boise
(208) 426-0778

Bigsmoke
8440 W. Fairview Ave.
Boise
(208) 323-8070

Hannifins Cigar
1024 W. Main St.
Boise
(208) 342-7473

Sturman's Smoke Shop
218 N. 10th St.
Boise
(208) 338-3225

The Smoke Shack
631 Broadway Ave. S.
Buhl
(208) 543-5588

Li'l Cinders Smoke Shop
2311 Overland Ave.
Burley
(208) 677-9957

Big Smoke
2408 Cleveland Blvd.
Caldwell
(208) 454-5671

Big Smoke
213 W. Appleway Ave., Ste. 1
Coeur d'Alene
(208) 667-2860

Bulldog Pipe and Cigar Co.
200 W. Hanley Ave.
Coeur d'Alene
(208) 762-4333

Fightin' Creek Smoke Shop
23181 S. Hwy. 95
Coeur d'Alene
(208) 676-0195

Prim's Smokeshoppe
416 E. Sherman Ave.
Coeur d'Alene
(208) 664-0786

Thunderbird Smoke Shop
50951 US Hwy. 95
Culdesac
(208) 843-2309

Pick and Pack
North Gayway Jct.
Fruitland
(208) 452-3134

Tobacco Hut
240 W. Hayden Ave.
Hayden
(208) 762-0704

Golden Crown Lounge
545 Shoup Ave.
Idaho Falls
(208) 522-9140

Dearden's Smoke Shop
1038 S. Lincoln Ave.
Jerome
(208) 324-6501

Purple Feather Smoke Shop
109 S. Main St.
Kooskia
(208) 926-7356

Webb Store Smoke Shop
30774 McCormack Ridge Rd.
Lapwai
(208) 843-2674

Big Smoke
West Hwy. 30
Meridian
(208) 888-5411

Big Smoke
730 W. Pullman Rd.
Moscow
(208) 882-7441

Big Smoke
305 American Legion Blvd.
Mountain Home
(208) 587-7354

Orofino Smoke Shop
10446 Hwy. 12
Orofino
(208) 476-4414

Main St. Tobacco
540 N. Main St.
Pocatello
(208) 478-2137

The Smoke Shack
74 S. Idaho St.
Wendell
(208) 536-6546

ILLINOIS
House of Tobacco
4511 Greenwood Court
Algonquin
(847) 854-4340

Abbey, The
6500 W. Main St.
Belleville
(618) 398-3176

Tobacco House
337 Kennedy Dr.
Bradley
(815) 932-6816

Tobacco House
1230 N. Kinzie Ave.
Bradley
(815) 933-7737

Jon's Pipe Shop
509 E. Green St.
Champaign
(217) 344-3459

Bohica Tobacco Lounge
5518 S. Archer Ave.
Chicago
(773) 581-0500

House of Hookah Lounge
607 W. Belmont Ave.
Chicago
(773) 348-1550

Iwan Ries & Co.
19 S. Wabash Ave.
Chicago
(312) 372-1306

Jorgio Cigar Inc.
320 S. Halsted St.
Chicago
(312) 906-9500

Shah & Parikh
14 E. Jackson Blvd.
Chicago
(312) 362-1608

TESA Cigar Co.
464 N. Halsted St.
Chicago
(312) 929-3075

Trading Post Tobacco & Cigars
5510 W. Devon Ave.
Chicago
(773) 763-8937

Up Down Cigar
1550 N. Wells St.
Chicago
(312) 337-8025

Utopia Cigars Inc.
6355 W. Montrose Ave.
Chicago
(773) 725-1810

Casa de Montecristo
1332 W. 55th St.
Countryside
(708) 352-6668

Elmhurst Cigar House
114 W. Park Ave.
Elmhurst
(630) 832-3030

Tobacco House
19985 S. La Grange Rd.
Frankfort
(815) 464-9230

Churchill & Burns
324 N. Main St.
Galena
(815) 777-2442

Republic Tobacco LP
2301 Ravine Way
Glenview
(847) 832-9700

Grayslake Tobacco Inc.
1864 E. Belvidere Rd.
Grayslake
(847) 548-0905

Bogie's Fine Cigars & Smoke
House
17816 Halsted St.
Homewood
(708) 798-4914

Smoke House
205 E. Morton Ave.
Jacksonville
(217) 243-1555

Tobacco Cheaper
1160 W. Morton Ave.
Jacksonville
(217) 245-4293

Cigars & More
314 S. Milwaukee Ave.
Libertyville
(847) 918-9999

Smoke House
318 W. Roosevelt Rd.
Lombard
(630) 691-8644

All About It Custom Glass and
Smoke Shop
1228 N. Green St.
McHenry
(815) 578-0659

Tobacco 4 Less
406 Nelson Rd.
New Lenox
(815) 485-6011

Arango Cigar Co.
3170 Commercial Ave.
Northbrook
(847) 480-0055

Habana Cigar House
2215 Algonquin Rd.
Rolling Meadows
(847) 517-4444

Friar Tuck Beverage
1333 Savoy Plaza Lane
Savoy
(217) 355-7933

Inferno Lounge
901 S. Roselle Rd.
Schaumburg
(847) 301-9999

X-hale
1320 N. Roselle Rd.
Schaumburg
(847) 884-6250

Tobacco House
8005 183rd St.
Tinley Park
(708) 444-4060

Eight To Eight Tobacco
300 E. Saint Charles Rd.
Villa Park
(630) 993-1234

Ultimate Cigar Smoke
137 E. North Ave.
Villa Park
(708) 431-4515

Smoke Shop
1203 Butterfield Rd.
Wheaton
(630) 752-9580

Cigary International Ltd.
139 Skokie Rd.
Wilmette
(847) 256-7676

INDIANA

Smoke House Inc.
378 W. Main St.
Austin
(812) 794-4560

Hardwicke's Pipe & Tobacco
743 Broad Ripple Ave.
Indianapolis
(317) 257-5915

High on the Hill
3729 W. 16th St.
Indianapolis
(317) 972-4455

Magic Bus
1073 Broad Ripple Ave.
Indianapolis
(317) 251-5463

Tobacco Shop
3854 Lafayette Rd.
Indianapolis
(317) 299-6010

Carmack's Cigar & Tobacco
   Shop
822 Logan St.
Noblesville
(317) 773-3770

Smoke House
60 S. Broadway
Peru
(765) 473-9917

IOWA

J T Connolly's Tobacco Bowl
111 S. Dubuque St.
Iowa City
(319) 338-5885

KANSAS

Smoke City
303 S. Wilson Ave.
Chanute
(620) 365-7993

Tobacco Row
1405 S. Santa Fe Ave.
Chanute
(620) 431-3371

Downtown Smoke Shop
115 E. 6th St.
Concordia
(785) 243-9730

Oyler Jimmie D
8375 Cedar Creek Rd.
DeSoto
(913) 583-3236

Fort Scott Smoke Shop
1705 S. National Ave.
Fort Scott
(620) 223-1441

Tommys Tobacco No. 102
110 N. 4th St.
Garden City
(620) 276-3803

Huff & Puff
130 E. Main St.
Gardner
(913) 884-6084

Smokers Outlet
3220 10th St.
Great Bend
(620) 792-7580

Tobacco-N-More
1103 Vine St.
Hays
(785) 625-3192

Smoke Stop
318 N. Plum St.
Hutchinson
(620) 669-1010

Smoker Friendly
1329 E. 4th Ave.
Hutchinson
(620) 665-6639

Tobacco Town
411 N. Adams St.
Hutchinson
(620) 665-3860

Tobacco Town
1813 W. Main St.
Independence
(620) 331-7766

Tobacco Rd.
205 W. 18th St.
Junction City
(785) 238-2128

Dunn's Pipe Tobacco & Gift
7640 State Ave.
Kansas City
(913) 788-5588

Smoke Easy
6000 Leavenworth Rd.
Kansas City
(913) 299-2264

Tobacco Road Smoke Shop
8155 State Ave.
Kansas City
(913) 334-4567

Centro Cigars
1520 Wakarusa Dr.
Lawrence
(785) 856-7773

Tobacco Express #1
2104 W. 25th St., Ste. A
Lawrence
(785) 842-0100

Tobacco Mart
1420 W. 23rd St.
Lawrence
(785) 830-9622

Smoke Hut at Doris' Market
111 N. Broadway St.
Leavenworth
(913) 682-2500

Black Dog
12815 W. 87th St. Pkwy.
Lenexa
(913) 495-5515

Tommy's Tobacco
612 S. Kansas Ave.
Liberal
(620) 624-9228

Tobacco Alley
1815 Ft. Riley Blvd.
Manhattan
(785) 770-3641

Smoker Friendly
720 W. Kansas Ave.
McPherson
(620) 241-8711

A & E Smoke Shop
110 N. Meridian Rd.
Newton
(316) 283-2279

Tee Pees Smoke Shop
301 W. 5th St.
Newton
(316) 283-4889

Tee Pees Smoke Shop
214 S. Kansas Ave.
Newton
(316) 284-9901

Smoke Hut
130 S. Clairborne Rd.
Olathe
(913) 829-9191

Cigar & Tabac Ltd.
6898 W. 105th St.
Overland Park
(913) 381-5597

Outlaw Cigar Co.
13700 Metcalf Ave.
Overland Park
(913) 814-9000

Smokers Outlet
1001 N. Pearl St.
Paola
(913) 294-3772

Smokers Outlet II
725 S. Silver St.
Paola
(816) 657-3066

Smoke 4 Less
1805 S. 9th St.
Salina
(785) 827-5979

Smoke Shack
Ste. B
Salina
(785) 820-8327

Lorillard Tobacco Co.
6422 Vista Dr.
Shawnee
(913) 441-0942

Midwest Cigar Co.
541 W. 119th St.
Shawnee Mission
(913) 451-7899

Churchill's
4025 S.W. Gage Center Dr.
Topeka
(785) 273-0102

Prime USA Inc.
1221 S.W. 21st St.
Topeka
(785) 232-8787

Smoke House
1834½ Topeka Blvd.
Topeka
(785) 232-2221

Smokers & Convenience
1237 S.W. Huntoon St.
Topeka
(785) 235-8266

Tobacco Town
4220 S.W. 21st St.
Topeka
(785) 271-5773

Tobacco Town
400 S.W. 29th St.
Topeka
(785) 266-7000

B K's Tobacco
708 W. Oklahoma Ave.
Ulysses
(620) 356-5536

Smoker's Choice LLC
620 N. G St.
Wellington
(620) 326-2545

Sidekix Party & Tobacco
   Shoppe
1012 Poplar St.
Wellsville
(785) 883-4710

Becky's Smoke Shop
4757 S. Hydraulic St.
Wichita
(316) 524-6360

Central Smoke Shop
2718 E. Central Ave.
Wichita
(316) 689-8865

Cigar Chateau & Gifts
10221 W. 21st St. N.
Wichita
(316) 729-4566

Cigar Chateau & Gifts
3049 N. Rock Rd.
Wichita
(316) 636-2433

Cigars Etc.
4800 W. Central Ave.
Wichita
(316) 944-2447

4 Aces Smoke & Liquor
707 N. Waco Ave.
Wichita
(316) 425-7676

Heat Cigar & Hookah Lounge
338 N. Rock Rd.
Wichita
(316) 260-8895

The Humidor Cigars and
   Lounge
8558 W. 21st St. N.
Wichita
(316) 440-4890

Jasmine's Tobacco
403 S. Hydraulic St.
Wichita
(316) 263-7055

Moore Mercedes
2425 S. Glendale St.
Wichita
(316) 652-0013

Old Town Cigars Inc.
800 E. 1st St. N.
Wichita
(316) 267-8744

Orion'z Outer Limits
1602 S. Seneca St.
Wichita
(316) 269-1167

Petes Smoke & Cigar
305 S. Greenwich Rd.
Wichita
(316) 688-0717

Sinches Liquor Smoke Shop
1620 S. Meridan Ave.
Wichita
(316) 943-7301

Shesha Tobacco Shop
4600 W. Kellogg
Wichita
(316) 941-9150

Smoker Friendly
6659 E. Harry St.
Wichita
(316) 944-1500

Tee Pee's Smoke Shop
1963 S. Broadway St.
Wichita
(316) 263-2922

Tee Pee's Smoke Shop
219 E. Murdock St.
Wichita
(316) 264-8477

Tee Pee's Smoke Shop
1701 S. Seneca St.
Wichita
(316) 262-2023

Tee Pee's Smoke Shop
913 E. Harry St.
Wichita
(316) 263-1542

Smoker's Choice LLC
1321 Main St.
Winfield
(620) 229-9555

KENTUCKY
Bo's Smoke Shop
700 Bloomfield Rd.
Bardstown
(502) 348-4880

Tobacco Patch
221 W. John Rowan Blvd.
Bardstown
(502) 348-9163

Bowling Green Pipe & Cigar
434 E. Main St.
Bowling Green
(270) 904-2285

US Tobacco Outlet
2320 Bypass Rd.
Brandenburg
(270) 422-5681

D & S Smoke Shop
321 S. Central Ave.
Campbellsville
(270) 465-9441

Tobacco Shack
2618 Concrete Rd.
Carlisle
(859) 289-8587

Covington Tobacco
301 W. 4th St.
Covington
(859) 291-2244

Crescent Springs Tobacco
535 Buttermilk Pike
Crescent Springs
(859) 426-5545

Tobacco Pouch Inc.
1313 E. Main St.
Cumberland
(606) 589-5459

Farmer's Tobacco Co.
636 US 27
Cynthiana
(859) 234-8500

Bo's Smoke Shop
1714 Perryville Rd.
Danville
(859) 936-0014

R & D Tobacco
66 Warsaw Ave.
Dry Ridge
(859) 824-9663

D & L Tobacco and More
456 S. Mulberry St.
Elizabethtown
(270) 766-1791

Danny's Tobacco
615 N. Main St.
Elizabethtown
(270) 737-1333

Tobacco & More
1050 N. Mulberry St.
Elizabethtown
(270) 763-0591

Straus Tobacconist
7753 Mall Rd.
Florence
(859) 647-8600

Marie's Smoke Shop
1601 S. Green St.
Glasgow
(270) 651-5536

Bo's Smoke Shop
50 Shawnee Dr.
Hodgenville
(270) 358-9837

Tobacco Barn
235 River Dr.
Irvine
(606) 723-7701

Bo's Smoke Shop
512 E. Hwy. 60
Irvington
(270) 547-5445

Ron's Tobacco & More
344 Stanford St.
Lancaster
(859) 792-2199

Bo's Smoke Shop
755 W. Broadway St., Ste. 222
Lawrenceburg
(502) 839-8226

Bo's Smoke Shop
709 E. Main St.
Lebanon
(270) 699-3704

Fayette Cigar Store Inc.
137 E. Main St.
Lexington
(859) 252-6267

Lexington Tobacco Store
3130 Pimlico Pkwy.
Lexington
(859) 272-1762

Lorillard Tobacco Co.
3151 Custer Dr.
Lexington
(859) 272-0855

Martin's Cigar Shop
2220 Nicholasville Rd.
Lexington
(859) 275-2197

Straus Tobacconist
410 W. Vine St.
Lexington
(859) 252-5142

Tobacco Connection III
535 N.W. New Circle Rd.
Lexington
(859) 294-0031

Tobacco Station Inc.
2331 Versailles Rd.
Lexington
(859) 455-9818

Tobacco Station Inc.
1412 Leestown Rd.
Lexington
(859) 252-4565

Ultimate Smoke Shop
921 Beaumont Centre Pkwy.
Lexington
(859) 223-7059

Tobacco Market
989 N. Laurel Rd.
London
(606) 878-6270

D & J Tobacco Inc.
104 W. Madison St.
Louisa
(606) 638-0902

A A Bluff Smoke Shop
2521 7th Street Rd.
Louisville
(502) 636-0073

Bardstown Smoking Shop
2309 Bardstown Rd.
Louisville
(502) 452-6606

Golden Smoke Shop
6501 Shepherdsville Rd.
Louisville
(502) 968-3366

Jimmy's Smoke Shop
3415 Bardstown Rd.
Louisville
(502) 479-7990

Kenwood Smoke Shop
802 W. Kenwood Dr.
Louisville
(502) 368-4994

Kremer's Smoke Shoppe
401 E. Jefferson St.
Louisville
(502) 584-3332

Oxmoor Smoke Shoppe Ltd.
7900 Shelbyville Rd.
Louisville
(502) 426-4706

Smoker's Corner
440 W. Market St.
Louisville
(502) 589-3060

Smoking Chicks
9807 3rd St. Rd.
Louisville
(502) 995-4700

Smoking World
127 E. Tenny Ave.
Louisville
(502) 961-0599

Tobacco House
2911 Preston Hwy.
Louisville
(502) 634-4479

Triple Crown Cigars
315 W. Woodlawn Ave.
Louisville
(502) 363-1973

Vault Liquor & Smokes
1270 Bardstown Rd.
Louisville
(502) 479-7666

Wild Cat Discount Tobacco
445 Old US Hwy. 52
Manchester
(606) 598-4665

Middlesboro Smoke Shop
110 N. 12th St.
Middlesboro
(606) 248-0100

KT's Smoke Shop
340 E. Waverly St.
Morganfield
(270) 389-3825

Bo's Smoke Shop
811 S. Main St.
Morgantown
(270) 526-4734

Bo's Smoke Shop
5971 Kentucky 2830
Owensboro
(270) 684-6588

Low Bobs Tobacco
310 Main St.
Owenton
(502) 484-3284

Barn
Old Hwy. 25
Pineville
(606) 337-6657

Super Smokes
922 Dixie Hwy. N.
Radcliff
(270) 351-2900

Halls Tobacco Store
457 Eastern Bypass
Richmond
(859) 626-7670

Margaret's Tobacco
   Warehouse
4920 Louisville Rd.
Salvisa
(859) 865-4009

J J's Smoke Shop Inc.
10611 Dixie Hwy.
Valley Station
(502) 935-7665

LOUISIANA
Churchill's
7949 Jefferson Hwy., #C
Baton Rouge
(225) 927-4211

Havana House of Cigars
676 Jefferson Hwy.
Baton Rouge
(504) 930-0309

Big Country Tobacco
10075 Hwy. 79
Bethany
(318) 938-9100

Smokey's
316 Cumberland St.
Bogalusa
(985) 735-7377

The Tobacco House
3055 E. Texas St.
Bossier City
(318) 746-7700

Jewel's Cigar and Briar Shop
201 N. New Hampshire St.
Covington
(985) 892-5746

The Cigar Merchant
1001 Coolidge Blvd.
Lafayette
(337) 233-9611

Piper's Haven
2480 W. Congress St.
Lafayette
(337) 235-4757

Cigar Specialist
4315 Common St.
Lake Charles
(337) 480-0201

Kershaw's Tobacco
501 N. Hwy. 171
Lake Charles
(337) 855-0061

Smoke Corner
100 Edwards St.
Mansfield
(318) 872-2791

Tobacco City
2420 Barataria Blvd.
Marrero
(504) 371-4243

Don Juan Cigars
3200 Severn Ave., #120
Metairie
(504) 549-8510

Smokers Paradise V
3412 Desiard St.
Monroe
(318) 345-3944

Cigar Factory New Orleans
206 Bourbon St.
New Orleans
(504) 568-0168

Crescent City Cigar Shop Inc.
730 Orleans Ave.
New Orleans
(504) 522-4427

Holy Smokes
533 Saint Louis St.
New Orleans
(504) 588-1811

Kingfish Cigars
631 Royal St.
New Orleans
(504) 523-1908

Mary Jane's Emporium
1229 Decatur St.
New Orleans
(504) 525-8004

Mary Jane's Emporium
4507 Magazine St.
New Orleans
(504) 891-6554

New Orleans Cigar Company
201 Saint Charles Ave.,
    Ste. 3315
New Orleans
(504) 524-9631

Players Pub
455 Hospital Rd.
New Roads
(225) 638-4588

Jade Tobacco Shop
805 E. Main St.
Oak Grove
(318) 428-4540

Apollo Tobacco
559 E. 70th St
Shreveport
(318) 868-3993

Brookshire's
3620 Pines Rd.
Shreveport
(318) 631-9610

Pipes Emporium
1304 Centenary Blvd.
Shreveport
(318) 424-2820

The Tobacco House
707 S. Pine St.
Vivian
(318) 375-2969

Mckenzie's Tobacco Shop
5875 Main St., Ste. J
Zachary
(225) 654-8010

MAINE

Bill Davis Tobacconists
166 Center St.
Auburn
(207) 795-1132

George's Smoke Shop
44 Alfred St.
Biddeford
(207) 282-7479

John's Smoke Shop
344 Main St.
Bingham
(207) 672-3500

Big Jack's Cigars
15 Commercial St.
Boothbay Harbor
(207) 633-4882

Jenney Station
105 Maine St.
Brunswick
(207) 725-6323

Kennebec Tobacco
124 Water St.
Hallowell
(207) 626-3350

Maine Smoke Shop
527 Stillwater Ave.
Old Town
(207) 827-5174

Maine Smoke Shop
804 Washington Ave.
Portland
(207) 879-4529

Maine Smoke Shop
618 US Rte. 1
Scarborough
(207) 883-4413

Carol's Pipes
Canaan Rd.
Skowhegan
(207) 474-8533

George's Smoke Shop
102 Water St.
Skowhegan
(207) 474-9883

Tip Top Tobacco Inc.
8 Madison Ave.
Skowhegan
(207) 474-9100

Calabash
425 Western Ave.
South Portland
(207) 774-8673

Waldoboro Smoke Shop
1530 Atlantic Hwy.
Waldoboro
(207) 832-7580

Joe's Smoke Shop
123 Main St.
Waterville
(207) 873-1280

Shakedown Street
33 N. Paris Rd.
West Paris
(207) 674-2047

MARYLAND

Annapolis Cigar Company
121 Main St.
Annapolis
(410) 295-7400

Ben Lex Tobacco
400 W. Lexington St.
Baltimore
(410) 837-1144

Firefly
3714 Eastern Ave.
Baltimore
(410) 732-1232

The Brick House
180 Winters Lane
Catonsville
(410) 788-5022

The Tobacco Barrel
1415 Merritt Blvd.
Dundalk
(410) 284-6777

Easton Cigar and Smoke Shop
6 Glenwood Ave.
Easton
(410) 770-5084

Davidus Cigars and Pipes
1015 W. Patrick St.
Frederick
(301) 662-6606

Tobacco Shack
Francis Scott Key Mall
Frederick
(301) 662-0553

Davidus Cigars Limited
15922 Shady Grove Rd.
Gaithersburg
(301) 963-8400

Tobacco Shack
12615 Wisteria Dr., Ste. D
Germantown
(301) 972-2905

Marley Tobacco
7900 Ritchie Hwy.,
    Marley Station Mall
Glen Burnie
(410) 590-2565

Cigar Locker
1740 Dual Hwy.
Hagerstown
(301) 739-8811

Marley Tobacco
7000 Arundel Mills Circle
Hanover
(410) 590-2565

Capital Plaza Smoke Shop
Capital Plaza
Landover
(301) 341-2614

Humidour Cigar Shoppe, The
10721 York Rd.
Cockeysville
(410) 666-3212

Zengars
8200 Perry Hall Blvd.
Nottingham
(410) 931-1299

Señor Cigar's
7809 Coastal Hwy.
Ocean City
(410) 524-2069

Fader's Tobacconist
Valley Village
Pikesville
(410) 363-7799

Chesapeake Cigars
11759 Somerset Ave.
Princess Anne
(410) 651-0522

House of Pipes
208 Main St.
Reisterstown
(410) 517-1177

One Flight Up
222 Main St.
Reisterstown
(410) 833-8575

Outerlimit Smoke Shop
7913 Pulaski Hwy.
Rosedale
(410) 238-1633

Other Side Inc.
15 W. Chesapeake Ave., #2
Towson
(410) 337-9202

MASSACHUSETTS

Brennan's Smoke Shop
308 Brockton Ave.
Abington
(781) 871-4388

Brennan's Smoke Shop
1035 Bedford St.
Abington
(781) 871-0221

Azon Cigars Inc.
378 Walnut St. Ext.
Agawam
(413) 301-0988

Cigar & Tobacco Emporium
965 Washington St.
Attleboro
(508) 399-9299

Luckys Smoke Shop
284 Cabot St.
Beverly
(978) 998-6145

David P. Ehrlich Co.
40 N. St.
Boston
(617) 227-1720

G. C. Tobacco
141 Tremont St.
Boston
(617) 338-8191

Gina Cigar Inc.
105 Kingston St.
Boston
(617) 426-4501

Gloucester Street Cigar Co.
34 Gloucester St.
Boston
(617) 424-1000

International News & Tobacco
Faneuil Hall Market Place
Boston
(617) 742-7457

Kang's Corner Gainsborough St.
56 Gainsborough St.
Boston
(617) 266-6876

L J Peretti Co.
2 Park Square
Boston
(617) 482-0218

Mary's Smoke Shop
36 Province St.
Boston
(617) 338-3011

99 Lobby Shop
99 High St.
Boston
(617) 482-2329

Nu Tobacco Store
404 Hanover St.
Boston
(617) 504-3096

Sid's Smoke
1124 Washington St.
Boston
(617) 350-6159

Sugar Daddy's Smoke Shop
472 Commonwealth Ave.
Boston
(617) 536-6922

Tedd's Tobacco Shop Inc.
57 Court St.
Boston
(617) 227-3387

Tobacco Treasurers
200 Seaport Blvd.
Boston
(617) 439-5498

Up in Smoke
176 Newbury St.
Boston
(617) 226-4400

Washington Smoke Shop
449 Washington St.
Boston
(617) 426-9779

Brennan's Smoke Shop
6 Broad St.
Bridgewater
(508) 697-9990

Happy Campah
51 Broad St.
Bridgewater
(508) 279-9995

Brennan's Smoke Shop
909 N. Main St.
Brockton
(508) 897-0777

Frye's Cigar Store
283 Main St.
Brockton
(508) 583-7338

Yogi Tobacco Inc.
200 Westgate Dr.
Brockton
(508) 583-9496

Jack's Smoke Shop
184 Alewife Brook Pkwy.
Cambridge
(617) 576-5583

Leavitt & Peirce Inc.
1316 Massachusetts Ave.
Cambridge
(617) 547-0576

C B Perkins
95 Washington St.
Canton
(781) 575-1411

Stogee's & Stuff
354 Turnpike St.
Canton
(781) 575-0759

Doyle's
285 Main St.
Charlestown
(617) 242-2002

Local Cigar Co.
705 Meadow St.
Chicopee
(413) 592-4141

Cigar's R Us
48 Maple St.
Danvers
(978) 739-9090

Courthouse Cigar Co.
366 Washington St.
Dedham
(781) 326-2400

Smoke Shop & More
216 Adams St.
Dorchester
(617) 436-8006

Tufts Tobacco
1006 Bennington St.
East Boston
(617) 561-8888

Blue Collar Cigar & Pipe Co.
35 Prospect St.
East Longmeadow
(413) 525-8522

Emporium
444 N. Main St.
East Longmeadow
(413) 525-0715

Guys Smoke Shop
423 Broadway
Everett
(617) 387-6691

Old Firehouse Smoke Shop
116 Rock St.
Fall River
(508) 678-2185

Murphy's Fine Wine Cigars
303 Main St.
Falmouth
(508) 540-7724

Garbarino D Co. Inc.
438 Waverly St.
Framingham
(508) 875-7242

Watch City Cigar
497 Worcester Rd.
Framingham
(508) 628-0112

Puff the Magic
649 Main St.
Hyannis
(508) 771-9090

Dragon's Leyr
285 Central St.
Leominster
(978) 466-5102

Highland Smoke Shop
132 Highland Ave.
Malden
(781) 397-7401

Pleasant Smoke
428 Main St.
Malden
(781) 321-3593

Tinder Box
11 Market St.
Mashpee
(508) 539-3303

Melting Pot
1647 Blue Hill Ave.
Mattapan
(617) 298-2288

Medford Square Smoke Shop
37 Riverside Ave.
Medford
(781) 395-2970

Tufts Square Tobacco
468 Main St.
Medford
(781) 391-1820

Old Cuban Cigar Co.
173 S. Main St.
Middleton
(978) 777-4129

Newton Smoke Shop
396 Watertown St.
Newton
(617) 527-3891

Cigar City
97 Bridge St.
North Weymouth
(781) 335-3113

Lizotte's Tobacco Shop
76 Main St.
Northampton
(413) 584-2812

Cigarman's Shop
181 W. Main St.
Norton
(508) 285-5900

Main Street Smoke Shop
7 Main St.
Peabody
(978) 532-8118

Brennan's Smoke Shop
95 Church St.
Pembroke
(781) 826-5773

Brennan's Smoke Shop
24 Main St.
Plymouth
(508) 746-5711

Brennan's of Quincy Square
1442 Hancock St.
Quincy
(617) 786-8610

Tobacco Treasures
1776 Heritage Dr.
Quincy
(617) 471-4540

Brennan's Smoke Shop
1510 US 44
Raynham
(508) 828-5773

ABC the Cigar Store
170 Revere St.
Revere
(781) 289-4959

Brennan's Smoke Shop
314 Union St.
Rockland
(781) 878-1347

Red Lion Smoke Shop
94 Washington St.
Salem
(978) 745-2050

Bill's Cigar Box East
111 Taunton Ave.
Seekonk
(508) 336-6577

City Cigarette Sales Inc.
130 Broadway
Somerville
(617) 666-4900

Robbins Cigar Co.
5 Davis Square
Somerville
(617) 625-6280

Schubert's
482 W. Broadway
South Boston
(617) 269-7137

Buckeye Bros Smokeshop/
    Harry's Caffe
974 Main St.
Springfield
(413) 731-6842

Victory Cigar Bar
615 Boston Post Rd.
Sudbury
(978) 443-4040

Mark's Smoke Shop & News
    Stand
360 Main St.
Wakefield
(781) 245-1211

Pinky Inc.
583 Main St.
Waltham
(781) 891-6281

Watch City Cigar Co.
853 Main St.
Waltham
(781) 891-6281

Brennan's Smoke Shop
208 Main St.
Wareham
(508) 295-5773

Jack's Smoke Shop
80 Main St.
Watertown
(617) 924-7772

S & A Smoke Shop
52 Mount Auburn St.
Watertown
(617) 923-2111

Chet's Smoke Shop
119 Main St.
Webster
(508) 943-9209

Tobacco Barn
53 Elm St.
Westfield
(413) 568-7286

Premium 70/70 Cigars
875 State Rd.
Westport
(508) 677-0333

Cigar Emporium
300 Mishawum Rd.
Woburn
(781) 933-0231

Beale St. News
16 Beale St.
Wollaston
(617) 471-9811

Michaels Cigar Bar
1 Exchange St.
Worcester
(508) 755-3866

Owl Shop Inc.
416 Main St.
Worcester
(508) 753-0423

Victory Bar & Cigar
56 Shrewsbury St.
Worcester
(508) 756-4747

MICHIGAN
Maison Edwards Tobacconist
11 Nickels Arcade
Ann Arbor
(734) 662-4145

Smoky's Fine Cigars
1423 E. Stadium Blvd.
Ann Arbor
(734) 222-0022

Stairway To Heaven
340 S. State St.
Ann Arbor
(734) 994-3888

Corona Smoke Shop
275 W. Columbia Ave.
Battle Creek
(269) 966-6670

Timothy's Fine Cigars
115 Center Ave.
Bay City
(989) 894-6673

Al's Smoke Shop
10808 Belleville Rd.
Belleville
(734) 697-5374

Tobacco Outfitters
13458 Northland Dr.
Big Rapids
(231) 527-2088

Smoker's Depot
10006 Grand River Rd.
Brighton
(810) 220-2701

Casa De Cuba
1235 S. Center Rd.
Burton
(810) 743-6050

H & I Smokers
42090 Ford Rd.
Canton
(734) 844-3003

Smokers Express
39749 Garfield Rd.
Clinton Township
(586) 412-0066

Don Yeyo Cigar Factory
22087 Michigan Ave.
Dearborn
(313) 563-2301

Telegraph Tobacco Inc.
544 N. Telegraph Rd.
Dearborn
(313) 274-8064

VIP Smokers Inc.
6800 Greenfield Rd.
Dearborn
(313) 581-9966

General Smoke Shop & Grocery
5436 W. Vernor Hwy.
Detroit
(313) 849-4000

M & M Tobacco Shop & More
LLC
8101 W. Vernor Hwy.
Detroit
(313) 554-9850

Renaissance 500 Tobacco
Shop
500 Renaissance Center
Detroit
(313) 259-6510

Star Light Smoke Shop Inc.
16155 Warren Ave. W.
Detroit
(313) 846-7702

Cigar Emporium
33185 Grand River Ave.
Farmington
(248) 426-7271

Capitol Cigar
24621 Halsted Rd.
Farmington Hills
(248) 474-5888

Smoker's Palace
3617 Corunna Rd.
Flint
(810) 424-0742

Smoke Break
6429 W. Pierson Rd.
Flushing
(810) 487-1415

Frankenmuth Cigar Co.
135 S. Franklin St.
Frankenmuth
(989) 652-0511

Quick Stop Smoke Shop
33259 Ford Rd.
Garden City
(734) 261-4955

Smoker's Palace
2213 E. Hill Rd.
Grand Blanc
(810) 695-3001

Admiral Discount Tobacco
1705 S. Beacon Blvd.
Grand Haven
(616) 850-0638

Buffalo Tobacco Traders
952 Fulton St. E.
Grand Rapids
(616) 451-8090

Smoke Shop
4301 Kalamazoo Ave. S.E.
Grand Rapids
(616) 647-5916

Admiral Discount Tobacco
300 Maplewood St.
Greenville
(616) 225-9950

Hill & Hill Tobacconists Ltd.
19529 Mack Ave.
Grosse Pointe Woods
(313) 882-9452

Smokers Depot of Highland
2862 E. Highland Rd.
Highland
(248) 889-6159

Cigar Ambassador
280 N. River Ave.
Holland
(616) 393-8160

Northern Michigan Tobacco
3087 W. Houghton Lake Dr.
Houghton Lake
(989) 366-7772

Smoker's Depot
1235 E. Grand River Ave.
Howell
(517) 546-2646

Smokers Palace X
1777 N. Van Dyke Rd.
Imlay City
(810) 724-0766

Smokey Mountain Tobacco LLC
2991 S. State Rd.
Ionia
(616) 522-9070

Corona Smoke Shop
305 Northwest Ave.
Jackson
(517) 782-1772

Red Arrow Cigar & Spirits
6980 Stadium Dr.
Kalamazoo
(269) 544-1220

Smoke Hut
3040 Portage St.
Kalamazoo
(269) 342-4201

Smokes on Burdick
1222 S. Burdick St.
Kalamazoo
(269) 383-6856

South Street Cigar & Wine
250 S. Kalamazoo Mall
Kalamazoo
(269) 385-8188

M I Tobacco World
4314 Division Ave. S.
Kentwood
(616) 530-7734

Tobacco Gallery
185 N. Park Blvd.
Lake Orion
(248) 693-6677

Smokers Oasis
4248 W. Saginaw Hwy.
Lansing
(517) 327-9900

Smokey Joe's II
5508 S. Cedar St.
Lansing
(517) 272-0155

Tobacco King
419 N. Clippert St.
Lansing
(517) 324-3433

Tobacco Gallery Inc.
3416 Fort St.
Lincoln Park
(313) 388-2277

Great Lakes Tobacco
34369 Plymouth Rd.
Livonia
(734) 266-0540

Smoky's Fine Cigars
16705 Middlebelt Rd.
Livonia
(734) 513-2622

Tobacco Shoppe
3114 N. Jefferson Ave.
Midland
(989) 835-9756

J & L Cigar Box
525 N. Main St.
Milford
(248) 685-3893

Cigars & Conversations LLC
45 S. Monroe St.
Monroe
(734) 241-7740

Indian River Tobacco Traders
8235 Mason Dr.
Newaygo
(231) 652-4500

Trader Tom's Tobacco Shop
43249 7 Mile Rd.
Northville
(248) 348-8333

A One Smoke Shop Inc.
30680 Beck Rd.
Novi
(248) 624-7018

Pete's Pipe & Tobacco
305 E. Mitchell St.
Petoskey
(231) 347-3322

La Casa De La Habana
470 Forest Ave.
Plymouth
(734) 207-9725

Cigar Rack
416 Huron Ave.
Port Huron
(810) 989-7225

Redford Tobacco Inc.
18950 Inkster Rd.
Redford
(313) 534-3333

Goodfellas Cigars Inc.
2944 Rochester Rd. S.
Rochester Hills
(248) 852-2111

Tobacco Outfitters
11555 Edgerton Ave. N.E.
Rockford
(616) 866-0049

Smokers Outlet
18655 E. 10 Mile Rd.
Roseville
(586) 773-5036

Smoky's Fine Cigars Royal Oak
303 S. Main St.
Royal Oak
(248) 546-3093

Butt Hut
3220 Bay Rd.
Saginaw
(989) 249-9130

Smoker's Palace
5206 Bay Rd.
Saginaw
(989) 799-9108

Smoking Post LLC
4040 Bay Rd.
Saginaw
(989) 249-0235

Lafayette Party Store
274 N. Lafayette St.
South Lyon
(248) 437-3666

Tobacco Road Inc.
620 N. Lafayette St.
South Lyon
(248) 486-7676

Churchills Fine Cigars
24545 W. 12 Mile Rd.
Southfield
(248) 948-9100

Smoke Shop Southfield
18248 W. 10 Mile Rd.
Southfield
(248) 200-0576

Southgate Tobacco Shop
13568 Eureka Rd.
Southgate
(734) 281-2972

Motor City Distributors Inc.
24200 Little Mack Ave.
St. Clair Shores
(586) 772-1400

Dodge Park Tobacco
38381 Dodge Park Rd.
Sterling Heights
(586) 978-7809

Smokers Express
44620 Mound Rd.
Sterling Heights
(586) 997-1900

Five Star Gifts & Smokers Shop
9061 Miller Rd.
Swartz Creek
(810) 635-4866

Nolan's Tobacconists
336 E. Front St.
Traverse City
(231) 946-2640

Smoker Express
2981 E. Big Beaver Rd.
Troy
(248) 689-1840

Smokers Outlet
5086 Rochester Rd. N.
Troy
(248) 528-8018

Tobacco Road Inc.
1148 E.W. Maple Rd.
Walled Lake
(248) 926-9266

Ryan Smoke Shop
29134 Ryan Rd.
Warren
(586) 751-1700

Smoke-N-More
21433 Schoenherr Rd.
Warren
(586) 778-8202

Smokers Outlet of Warren
31900 Ryan Rd.
Warren
(586) 983-3777

Westland Smoke Shop
8335 N. Wayne Rd.
Westland
(734) 421-1570

Village Smoke Shop
2600 Benstein Rd.
Wolverine Lake
(248) 624-5330

Smoker Express
1799 E. Washtenaw Ave.
Ypsilanti
(734) 480-9620

MINNESOTA
Tobacco Valley
7546 149th St. W.
Apple Valley
(952) 431-3000

Tobacco Super Store
501 Paul Bunyan Dr. N.W.
Bemidji
(218) 444-9776

Oxboro Tobacco Inc.
9860 Lyndale Ave. S.
Bloomington
(952) 887-2085

Tobacco Den–Brainerd
627 Washington St.
Brainerd
(218) 822-3550

B C Tobacco
6930 Brooklyn Blvd.
Brooklyn Center
(763) 566-3366

Marcatomas Inc.
6288 Lakeland Ave. N.
Brooklyn Park
(763) 536-0332

Burn Premium Cigar
    Specialists
409 W. Burnsville Pkwy.
Burnsville
(952) 808-9259

Lorillard Tobacco Co.
208 River Ridge Circle N.
Burnsville
(952) 894-2238

Cigars Unlimited
2950 Coon Rapids Blvd. N.W.
Coon Rapids
(763) 323-0752

Tobacco Unlimited
133 85th Ave. N.W.
Coon Rapids
(763) 786-5420

Tobacco Plus Inc.
8461 E. Point Douglas Rd. S.
Cottage Grove
(651) 459-4091

Andy's Cigar Shop Walk In
County Rd. 3 & County Rd. 66
Crosslake
(218) 692-3722

DL Tobacco
611 Washington Ave.
Detroit Lakes
(218) 847-3883

Butts Smoke Shop
5610 Grand Ave.
Duluth
(218) 628-1502

Duluth Tobacco & Gifts
11 N. 4th Ave. W.
Duluth
(218) 722-2229

Electric Fetus
12 E. Superior St.
Duluth
(218) 722-9970

Last Place On Earth
120 E. Superior St.
Duluth
(218) 727-1244

Smoke Shop
1405 Miller Trunk Hwy.
Duluth
(218) 724-9728

Eagan Cigars & Tobacco Store
3450 Pilot Knob Rd.
Eagan
(651) 454-2475

Eagan Tobacco
1960 Cliff Lake Rd.
Eagan
(651) 686-2990

Al's Smoke Shop
19112 Freeport St N.W. #157
Elk River
(763) 241-8322

Chapman St. Books & Prairie
    Fire Tobacco
139 E. Chapman St.
Ely
(218) 365-2212

Excelsior Vintage Inc.
378 Oak St.
Excelsior
(952) 401-0346

Tobacco
315 Osborne Rd. N.E.
Fridley
(763) 792-2074

Tobacco Den
70 S.E. 7th St.
Grand Rapids
(218) 327-8964

Range Tobacco Inc.
121 E. Howard St.
Hibbing
(218) 263-7519

Back Door Tobacco
813 Main St.
Hopkins
(952) 933-3377

U.S. Tobacco
520 Blake Rd. N.
Hopkins
(952) 933-0133

Good Life
90 Mahtomedi Ave.
Mahtomedi
(651) 429-7841

Professor Pipes & Stuff
418 S. Front St.
Mankato
(507) 386-0182

Smokers House
13543 Grove Dr.
Maple Grove
(763) 494-3050

Tobacco Grove
8063 Wedgewood Lane N.
Maple Grove
(763) 494-6688

Bloomington Smoke Shop
10619 France Ave. S.
Minneapolis
(612) 277-0975

Buzz Tobacco
8189 University Ave. N.E.
Minneapolis
(763) 784-9092

Clown Glass
2114 S. Lyndale Ave.
Minneapolis
(612) 870-6211

Downtown Tobacco
10 5th St. N.
Minneapolis
(612) 332-9506

Emporium Exceptionale
5601 W. 78th St.
Minneapolis
(952) 835-9298

46th & Nicollet Tobacco
4614 Nicollet Ave.
Minneapolis
(612) 824-4305

GM Tobacco
2927 26th Ave. S.
Minneapolis
(612) 728-8085

Golden Leaf Ltd.
3032 Hennepin Ave.
Minneapolis
(612) 824-1867

Lewis Pipe & Tobacco
527 Marquette Ave.
Minneapolis
(612) 332-9129

Lyndale Tobacco
703 W. Lake St.
Minneapolis
(612) 354-3468

My Tobacco Store
785 45th Ave. N.E.
Minneapolis
(763) 571-5583

Peacemaker
2414 Hennepin Ave.
Minneapolis
(612) 377-3345

Royal Cigar Tobacco
403 14th Ave. S.E.
Minneapolis
(612) 331-7250

Royal Tobacco
5625 Xerxes Ave. N.
Minneapolis
(763) 566-2277

Sarna's Tobacco Depot
2501 University Ave. N.E.
Minneapolis
(612) 782-6940

Tobacco King
1444 85th Ave. N.
Minneapolis
(763) 585-8960

Uptown Tobacco Shop
2536 Hennepin Ave.
Minneapolis
(612) 377-5139

Cigar Lounge
4785 County Rd. 101
Minnetonka
(952) 933-8454

Tobacco Store
13025 Ridgedale Dr.
Minnetonka
(952) 545-0707

Monty Tobacco
1220 Hwy. 25 S.
Monticello
(763) 295-5005

Mellow Mood Pipe & Tobacco
1825 Main Ave.
Moorhead
(218) 233-3161

New Hope Smoke Shop Inc.
2767 Winnetka Ave.
New Hope
(763) 540-9355

Tiny's
321 Division St. S.
Northfield
(507) 645-6862

Crooks Smoke Shop
2461 Sioux Trail N.W.
Prior Lake
(952) 445-4708

Ramsey Smoke Shop
14050 Saint Francis Blvd.
Ramsey
(763) 323-1444

Golden Tobacco
22 W. 66th St.
Richfield
(612) 869-5551

Ike's Gift Shop Inc.
2306 W. 66th St.
Richfield
(612) 866-3166

Smoke Shop
4080 W. Broadway Ave.
Robbinsdale
(763) 535-6866

Tobacco Tree Inc.
1734 Lexington Ave. N.
Roseville
(651) 489-4028

Smoke Shop Super Store
1227 Timberlane Dr.
Sauk Centre
(320) 352-5921

Tobacco Express Inc.
1148 Vierling Dr. E.
Shakopee
(952) 233-1564

Smoke Shop
1501 1st St. S.
St. Cloud
(320) 654-1729

Abe's Tobacco
2303 White Bear Ave. N.
St. Paul
(651) 779-0500

Arden Hills Tobacco
3673 Lexington Ave. N.
St. Paul
(651) 766-8885

Beyond & Tobacco
898 Arcade St.
St. Paul
(651) 772-3333

Jonathon Robert Fielding & Co.
1767 Lexington Ave. N.
St. Paul
(651) 489-7504

Jubilee St Maries
101 5th St. E.
St. Paul
(651) 224-4579

Midway Tobacco Marketplace
1418 University Ave. W.
St. Paul
(651) 644-3701

Midway Tobacco Smokes
1464 University Ave. W.
St. Paul
(651) 647-5333

Mr Nice Guy
1412 White Bear Ave. N.
St. Paul
(651) 739-1965

Oakdale Tobacco Inc.
7157 10th St. N.
St. Paul
(651) 738-9511

Slik's Smoke & Snack Shop
55 5th St. E
St. Paul
(651) 767-8677

Smokers Oasis
6084 12th St. N.
St. Paul
(651) 739-1871

Smokes 4 Less
1700 Rice St.
St. Paul
(651) 489-1867

Smokie's Tobacco Discount
  Outlet
1704 Suburban Ave.
St. Paul
(651) 776-8426

Southview Tobacco Inc.
227 13th Ave. S.
St. Paul
(651) 455-1632

Stogies on Grand
961 Grand Ave.
St. Paul
(651) 222-8700

Stillwater Tobacco
2040 Market Dr.
Stillwater
(651) 351-9614

Smoke Shop
136 2nd St. S.
Waite Park
(320) 252-5434

Smoke Shop Super Store
43 Waite Ave. N.
Waite Park
(320) 253-4658

Cigar Jones Inc.
17643 Minnetonka Blvd.
Wayzata
(952) 475-3131

Perfect Ash—That Tobacco
  Place
809 Sibley Memorial Hwy.
West St. Paul
(651) 457-4953

Smokeshop II
929 Wildwood Rd.
White Bear Lake
(651) 773-8220

Smokes For Less
415 1st St. S.
Willmar
(320) 235-0593

MISSISSIPPI

Epitome
2600 Beach Blvd.
Biloxi
(228) 388-2022

Mack's Tobacco Shop
6 Overby St.
Brandon
(601) 824-0507

Tobacco Market
115 Village Square Dr.
Brandon
(601) 992-2882

Tobacco Mart
207 US 51
Brookhaven
(601) 833-0085

Dar's Smoke Shop
8017 Hwy. 178
Byhalia
(662) 838-3910

Tobacco Shack
10340 Diberville Blvd.
Diberville
(228) 396-3666

Tobacco Market
2990 Old Hwy. 49 S.
Florence
(601) 845-4707

B & B Tobacco Butts & Brew
 Inc.
4307 Lakeland Dr.
Flowood
(601) 932-2739

Lorillard Tobacco Co.
513 Liberty Rd.
Flowood
(601) 932-8070

Baldy's Cigar
2510 14th St.
Gulfport
(228) 314-5069

Wigley & Culp Inc.
1535 29th Ave.
Gulfport
(228) 864-2092

Tobacco Stores
3901 Hardy St.
Hattiesburg
(601) 450-2558

Tobacco Shack
1401 W. Goodman Rd.
Horn Lake
(662) 393-2485

Southern Tobacco Co.
180 Aberdeen Rd.
Houston
(662) 456-5111

Corr-Williams Co.
110 Airport Rd., Ste. B
Jackson
(601) 420-4314

Country Squire
1855 Lakeland Dr.
Jackson
(601) 362-2233

Habana Smoke Shoppe
4760 I-55 N., Suite #A
Jackson
(601) 713-0010

Joe Malick Tobacco
Jackson
(601) 922-4292

Tobacco Shop
17343 Hwy. 603
Kiln
(228) 255-7772

Dan's Discount
615 N. 16th Ave.
Laurel
(601) 426-3848

Wigley & Culp Inc.
50 Allman St.
Lucedale
(601) 947-8186

Tobacco Depot
7852 US Hwy. 11
Lumberton
(601) 796-8701

Tobacco Market
501 Pinola Dr.
Magee
(601) 849-2350

Tobacco World
2440 N. Hills St.
Meridian
(601) 693-6751

Tobacco World
93 S. Frontage Rd.
Meridian
(601) 484-7171

Tobacco Mart
3 Government Fleet Rd.
Natchez
(601) 304-2037

Tobacco Station
281 John R Junkin Dr.
Natchez
(601) 442-0147

Smoke Shop LLC
303 E. Bankhead St.
New Albany
(662) 534-4800

Pugs 1
6213 Washington Ave.
Ocean Springs
(228) 818-0848

Dot's Tobacco
5715 Telephone Rd.
Pascagoula
(228) 696-8688

2 Back-O-Town
16829 Kapalama Rd
Pass Christian
(228) 586-6244

Shirley & Malcolm Smoke Shop
105 Choctaw Town Ctr.
Philadelphia
(601) 656-9944

Tobacco World
250 W. Beacon St.
Philadelphia
(601) 389-1135

Tobacco Shack 3
803 Memorial Blvd.
Picayune
(601) 798-9250

Tobacco Shop
282 W. Oxford St.
Pontotoc
(662) 488-0220

Tobacco Shack
1233 S. Main St.
Poplarville
(601) 795-9060

Tammy's Tobacco Town
1201 Old Hwy. 49 S.
Richland
(601) 420-5186

Tobacco 2 Go
17480 Hwy. 21
Sebastopol
(601) 625-0202

Cedar Point Tobacco Store
1046 Church Rd. W.
Southaven
(662) 280-7868

Doc's Tobacco Outlet & Pagers
989 US 61 Bsn.
Vicksburg
(601) 636-4176

Joseph Malick Tobacco Co.
1620 Cherry St.
Vicksburg
(601) 636-3971

Smoke Stack, The
206 W. Main St.
West Point
(662) 494-5774

T and S Smoke Shop
1025 Jerry Clower Blvd.
Yazoo City
(662) 746-8844

MISSOURI
Havana Cigar Room
3868 Vogel Rd.
Arnold
(636) 282-2975

Smoke Shop
1389 Jeffco Blvd.
Arnold
(636) 296-5523

Town & Country Tobacco
13933 Manchester Rd.
Ballwin
(636) 227-0707

Tobacco Row Smoke Shop
264 N.E. Elm St.
Billings
(417) 744-8574

TC's Liquor Locker & Smoke
   Shops Inc.
321 E. Airport Dr.
Carthage
(417) 358-2992

Cigar Box, The
240 Long Rd.
Chesterfield
(636) 536-4949

Tobakko's
17205 Chesterfield Airport Rd.
Chesterfield
(636) 536-0606

Aardvarx
17 N. 10th St.
Columbia
(573) 874-8600

Dreams Smoke Shop
101 E. Walnut St.
Columbia
(573) 449-8502

Nostalgia Shop
2600 S. Providence Rd.
Columbia
(573) 874-1950

Tinder Box International
2703 E. Broadway
Columbia
(573) 256-5363

Captain Z's
520 Bailey Rd.
Crystal City
(636) 933-0761

Smokey's Place Inc.
2031 Rock Rd.
DeSoto
(636) 586-2855

Cheapy Smokes
236 Axminister Dr.
Fenton
(636) 343-0079

Dirt Cheap Cigarettes & Beer
1119 Gravois Rd.
Fenton
(636) 349-7710

Hypnotized Smoke Shop Inc.
2967 Patterson Rd.
Florissant
(314) 972-1437

Tinder Box
147 Jamestown Mall
Florissant
(314) 741-0899

Havannibal Cigar Co.
308 Broadway
Hannibal
(573) 629-1616

Inhale
7211 N. Lindbergh Blvd.
Hazelwood
(314) 731-4241

Smokin J's
1753 Halifax Rd.
Holts Summit
(573) 896-8900

Dragon Lair Inc.
4591 Main St.
House Springs
(636) 375-0003

Smoke Shop, The
931 US 50 Bsn.
Jefferson City
(573) 761-7405

Welcome Smokers
2111 Route C
Jefferson City
(573) 635-7045

Diebel's Sportsmens Gallery
426 Ward Pkwy.
Kansas City
(816) 931-2988

Havana Moon Inc.
1614 W. 39th St.
Kansas City
(816) 756-3367

Head Space on Troost
4254 Troost Ave.
Kansas City
(816) 931-4833

It's A Dream Smoke Shop
3942 Broadway St.
Kansas City
(816) 753-5733

Main Street Tobacco & Gifts
4307 Main St.
Kansas City
(816) 531-4441

Outlaw Cigar Co.
6234 N. Chatham Ave.
Kansas City
(816) 505-2442

Osage Cigar Co.
4398 Hwy. 54
Osage Beach
(515) 302-7670

Smoke Shack
9742 Lackland Rd.
Overland
(314) 426-4042

Smoke Shop
11086 Midland Blvd.
Overland
(314) 427-5006

Jasper's Smoke Shop
2018 Lake Dr.
Perryville
(573) 517-7883

Smoke Shop
105 Port Perry Dr.
Perryville
(573) 547-5056

Red-X
2401 N.W. Platte Rd.
Riverside
(816) 741-3377

Mule Trading Post & Tobacco
 Barn, The
11132 Dillon Outer Rd.
Rolla
(573) 341-0162

Colony Tobacco
1948 S. Stewart Ave.
Springfield
(417) 883-0662

Cosmic Fish
1437 S. Glenstone Ave.
Springfield
(417) 883-4090

Discount Tobacco Shop Inc.
3167 W. Republic Rd.
Springfield
(417) 889-9737

Just For Him
1334 E. Battlefield Rd.
Springfield
(417) 886-8380

Tobacco World
1420 S. Glenstone Ave.
Springfield
(417) 890-1978

John Dengler Tobacconist
700 S. Main St.
St. Charles
(636) 946-6899

Lorillard Tobacco Co.
192 Hughes Lane
St. Charles
(636) 947-1431

Basement
5025 Lemay Ferry Rd.
St. Louis
(314) 487-3980

Brennan's
4659 Maryland Ave.
St. Louis
(314) 361-9444

Briars & Blends Cigar Shop
   Ltd.
6405 Hampton Ave.
St. Louis
(314) 351-1131

Cheapy Smokes
5243 Southwest Ave.
St. Louis
(314) 772-7222

Cool Smoke
10544 Page Ave.
St. Louis
(314) 428-6789

Emporium
556 Limit Ave.
St. Louis
(314) 721-6277

Hill Cigar
5360 Southwest Ave.
St. Louis
(314) 645-1045

HSB Tobacconist
6362 Delmar Blvd.
St. Louis
(314) 721-1483

J R Cigars
4 N. Central Ave.
St. Louis
(314) 727-5667

Jon's Pipe Shop
42 N. Central Ave.
St. Louis
(314) 721-1480

Lit Cigars
7919 Big Bend Blvd.
St. Louis
(314) 968-4858

Smoke Land
9495 Olive Blvd.
St. Louis
(314) 432-1540

Top Hat Tobacco
124 W. Jefferson Ave. 107
St. Louis
(314) 966-1002

Victor & Carelene Distribu-
   tion Inc.
8807 Natural Bridge Rd.
St. Louis
(314) 427-6758

Welcome Smokers
67 Grasso Plaza
St. Louis
(314) 631-0746

Tinder Box
6227 Mid Rivers Mall Dr.
St. Peters
(636) 441-0994

MONTANA
Friendly Smoker
1246 Central Ave.
Billings
(406) 248-9288

Smoker Friendly
2646 Grand Ave.
Billings
(406) 651-9118

Smoker Friendly
2750 Old Hardin Rd.
Billings
(406) 248-2689

Smoker Friendly
251 Main St.
Billings
(406) 254-6166

Stogies
2717 1st Ave. N.
Billings
(406) 248-6879

Tobacco Country
1500 Broadwater Ave.
Billings
(406) 652-8455

Tobacco Row
2450 King Ave. W.
Billings
(406) 656-1188

Tobacco Row
655 Main St.
Billings
(406) 252-1558

Coldsmoke Tobacco
8 N. 9th Ave.
Bozeman
(406) 556-8444

Smokin Smitty's
2742 W. Main St.
Bozeman
(406) 220-3363

Cigarero Cigar Shop
9 N. Main St.
Butte
(406) 723-7612

Gilligan's Tobacco Shop Inc.
916 E. Front St.
Butte
(406) 723-6900

Smoke Ridge
1380 Hwy. 220
Choteau
(406) 466-5952

Smokers Friendly
5345 US Hwy. 2 W.
Columbia Falls
(406) 892-1555

Sherlock's Home
2920 10th Ave. S.
Great Falls
(406) 761-1680

Smokers Express
1423 8th Ave. N.
Great Falls
(406) 454-9046

Smoker Friendly
700 2nd St.
Havre
(406) 265-4377

Capital City Perks
9 N. Last Chance Gulch St.
Helena
(406) 442-6424

Man Store
615 Helena Ave.
Helena
(406) 443-8084

Man Store
200 N. Montana Ave.
Helena
(406) 227-6519

Smoker Friendly
1425 11th Ave.
Helena
(406) 442-1015

Heads Up Tobacco Acc
2680 US Hwy. 2 E.
Kalispell
(406) 257-0091

Smoke Shack
1502 Minnesota Ave.
Libby
(406) 293-2931

Smoker Friendly
115 N. 7th St.
Miles City
(406) 234-8203

Bell Pipe & Tobacco Shoppe
136 E. Broadway St.
Missoula
(406) 728-2781

Urban Kings
103 E. Main St.
Missoula
(406) 549-0626

Huff N Puff Inc.
PO Box 577
Park City
(406) 633-2393

Dupuis Smoke Signal
5 Terrace Lake Rd. E.
Ronan
(406) 676-8181

NEBRASKA
Classic Cigars by Meier's
S 13th St. & South St.
Lincoln
(402) 476-1518

Jake's Cigars
114 N. 14th St.
Lincoln
(402) 435-8117

Smokes'n Jokes
5560 S. 48th St., Ste. 2
Lincoln
(402) 420-5711

Tobacco Hut
4011 Harrison St.
Omaha
(402) 733-1527

NEVADA
Carson Cigar Co.
318 North Carson St.
Carson City
(775) 884-4402

Elko Smoke Shop
Silver Eagle Rd.
Elko
(775) 777-1732

Fox Peak Station
615 E. Williams Ave.
Fallon
(775) 423-5655

Hawaiian Smoke Shop
565 Marks St.
Henderson
(702) 248-2442

Man Cave Cigar Lounge
855 7 Hills Dr.
Henderson
(702) 478-8007

Palm Smoke & Gift
565 College Dr.
Henderson
(702) 568-6140

Smoke Plus
4608 E. Sunset Rd.
Henderson
(702) 454-8284

Smoke Shop
25 W. Army St.
Henderson
(702) 568-8988

Casa Fuente Cigars
3500 Las Vegas Blvd. S.
Las Vegas
(702) 731-5051

Cubinican Cigars
4750 W. Sahara Ave.
Las Vegas
(702) 878-8225

D & D Smoke Shop
3955 E. Owens Ave.
Las Vegas
(702) 251-7788

Don Pablo Cigar Co.
3049 Las Vegas Blvd. S.
Las Vegas
(702) 369-1818

Don Yeyo Cigar Factory
328 W. Sahara Ave.
Las Vegas
(702) 384-9262

Gorilla Radio Smoke Shop
4225 S. Eastern Ave.
Las Vegas
(702) 818-4400

Grand Havana House of Cigars
3645 Las Vegas Blvd. S.
Las Vegas
(702) 967-4300

Havana Cigar
3900 Paradise Rd.
Las Vegas
(702) 892-9555

Havana Honeys Cigars
4325 Industrial Rd., Ste. 315
Las Vegas
(702) 369-1100

Jays Smoke & Gift Shop
3266 Las Vegas Blvd. N.
Las Vegas
(702) 310-4093

Jaz's Smoke Shop & Mini Mart
5643 W. Charleston Blvd.
Las Vegas
(702) 822-1891

JIT Smoke Shop
4250 E. Bonanza Rd.
Las Vegas
(702) 438-5130

Las Vegas Cigar Lounge
5825 W. Sahara Ave.
Las Vegas
(702) 367-2284

Las Vegas Paiute Tribal Smoke
  Shop
1225 N. Main St.
Las Vegas
(702) 387-6433

Mr Smoke Shop
4640 Paradise Rd.
Las Vegas
(702) 650-0875

Mr. Bill's Pipe and Tobacco Co.
7460 W. Cheyenne Ave.
Las Vegas
(702) 214-6840

Natural Mystic
2307 Las Vegas Blvd. S.
Las Vegas
(702) 796-4367

Phils Cigar Co.
1000 S. Rampart Blvd.
Las Vegas
(702) 946-5100

Rick's Smoke Shop
2595 S. Maryland Pkwy.
Las Vegas
(702) 737-0655

Rick's Smoke Shop
8174 Las Vegas Blvd. S.
Las Vegas
(702) 737-7425

Sam's Smoke Shop
2486 E. Desert Inn Rd.
Las Vegas
(702) 765-9500

Smoke Shop
586 S. Decatur Blvd.
Las Vegas
(702) 258-0976

Smoke Shop & Body Jewelry
3300 E. Flamingo Rd.
Las Vegas
(702) 221-7161

Smoke Shop N Cigars
4985 W. Tropicana Ave.
Las Vegas
(702) 873-4002

Still Smoking
2605 S. Decatur Blvd.
Las Vegas
(702) 227-3021

Summerlin Smoke Shop
2263 N. Rampart Blvd.
Las Vegas
(702) 838-3949

Tobacco Leaf
7175 W. Lake Mead Blvd.
Las Vegas
(702) 432-3000

Vegas Smoke Shop
3155 N. Rancho Dr.
Las Vegas
(702) 396-7259

Xclusive Cigars
6485 S. Rainbow Blvd.
Las Vegas
(702) 856-3120

Knight Smoke & Gift Shop
5960 Losee Rd.
North Las Vegas
(702) 639-4438

FUMARE
907 W. Moana Lane
Reno
(775) 825-1121

Silver Smoke
143 N. Virginia St.
Reno
(775) 348-4666

Tinder Box
4991 S. Virginia St.
Reno
(775) 826-2680

Reno-Sparks Indian Smoke
Shop
1962 Pyramid Way
Sparks
(775) 353-2140

Sun Valley Smoke Shop
5476 Sun Valley Blvd.
Sun Valley
(775) 674-1900

NEW HAMPSHIRE
Blowin' Smoke
132 Bedford Center Rd.,
Rte. 101
Bedford
(603) 472-5878

Capital Tobacco
75 S. Main St.
Concord
(603) 224-5001

Castro's Back Room
5 Depot St.
Concord
(603) 225-6522

Potente Cigars Inc.
308 Village St.
Concord
(603) 753-0037

Dave's Cigar Shop
35 6th St.
Dover
(603) 743-1442

Smoke Signals Pipe & Tobacco
3 Main St.
Dover
(603) 742-7473

Top Shelf Cigar Co.
96 Calef Hwy.
Epping
(603) 679-2447

Smoke N Barley
612 North Rd.
Franklin
(603) 524-5004

Twins Smoke Shop
1275 Hooksett Rd.
Hooksett
(603) 622-8946

C C & H Cigars
41 Central Square
Keene
(603) 352-3777

Happy Jack Pipe & Tobacco
   Shop
71 Church St.
Laconia
(603) 528-4092

Twins Smoke Shop
128 Rockingham Rd.
Londonderry
(603) 421-0242

Captain's Pleasure
990 Elm St.
Manchester
(603) 623-3739

Castro's Back Room
972 Elm St.
Manchester
(603) 606-7854

Goodtimes Smoke Shop
817 Elm St.
Manchester
(603) 647-0866

NH Cigars—Holy Smokes Cigars
297 S. Willow St.
Manchester
(888) 302-4427

Yessah Smoke Shop
260 Elm St.
Milford
(603) 672-0330

Castro's Back Room
119 Main St.
Nashua
(603) 881-7703

Goodtimes Smoke Shop &
   Emporium
449 Amherst St.
Nashua
(603) 886-0224

Smok'in Deals
112 Daniel Webster Hwy.
Nashua
(603) 888-7719

Two Guys Smoke Shop
15 Spit Brook Rd.
Nashua
(603) 891-2122

Newshop of Portsmouth
50 Fox Run Rd.
Newington
(603) 431-5665

Talking Heads Smoke Shop &
   Adult Novelties
51 John Stark Hwy.
Newport
(603) 863-7004

Village Cigar Emporium
3425 White Mountain Hwy.
North Conway
(603) 356-7755

Steele's
40 Main St.
Peterborough
(603) 924-7203

Cigars Etc. Inc.
9 Plaistow Rd.
Plaistow
(603) 382-3636

Federal Cigar
22 Ladd St.
Portsmouth
(603) 436-5363

Federal Cigar Too
2968 Lafayette Rd.
Portsmouth
(603) 436-3150

Smoke Stack Shop LLC
14 N. Main St.
Rochester
(603) 332-2486

Two Guys Smoke Shop
304 S. Broadway
Salem
(603) 898-2221

Village Tobacconist
Salem
(603) 448-7090

Gold Leaf Tobacconist
255 Lafayette Rd.
Seabrook
(603) 474-7744

Seacoast Cigar & Accessories
5 Main St.
Seabrook
(603) 474-1991

Smoke Ring
178 Lafayette Rd.
Seabrook
(603) 474-8999

Two Guys Smoke Shop
741 Lafayette Rd.
Seabrook
(603) 474-8222

Up In Smoke
919 Lafayette Rd.
Seabrook
(603) 760-7244

Smoke N Barley
485 Laconia Rd.
Tilton
(603) 524-5004

Un Dun
1 S. Main St.
West Lebanon
(603) 298-7028

Dulce Vida LLC
P.O. Box 602
West Swanzey
(603) 355-1255

NEW JERSEY
Tobacco Road
690 E. Bay Ave.
Barnegat
(609) 698-1944

Crossroads Sweet Shoppe
62 Broad St.
Bloomfield
(973) 748-5930

Sanj's Smoke Shop
419 Broad St.
Bloomfield
(973) 743-0693

Ashes to Ashes
300 Farnsworth Ave.
Bordentown
(609) 298-2727

Cigars Plus
2140 Route 88
Brick
(732) 295-9795

Up in Smoke Cigars
421 Washington St.
Cape May
(609) 884-5009

Churchill's Tobacco Shop Inc.
1201 Kings Hwy. N.
Cherry Hill
(856) 428-7361

Light 'N Up Cigars Premier
2089 Marlton Pike E.
Cherry Hill
(856) 424-3677

Puff & Stuff
21 North Ave E.
Cranford
(908) 272-6989

130 Smoke Shop
2900 Route 130
Delran
(856) 829-2929

Neros Cigars
421 N. Haddon Ave.
Haddonfield
(856) 428-0553

Lighthouse Cigars
1350 State Route 36
Hazlet
(732) 888-8118

Smoke Shop Xtreem
88 Broad St.
Keyport
(732) 264-1900

Nobles Smoke Shop
629 US 9
Lanoka Harbor
(609) 242-8744

Tobacco Leaf
3349-65 Route 1 S.
Lawrenceville
(609) 936-1400

Wonderland Smoke Shop
2793 Brunswick Pike
Lawrenceville
(609) 323-7473

Cigar Emporium
607 Ridge Rd.
Lyndhurst
(201) 438-8760

Hemingways Cigar Shop LLC
107 Merchants Way
Marlton
(856) 985-7580

Old Stogie
4 N. Maple Ave.
Marlton
(856) 983-6440

Smoker's Haven
952 State Route 34 #3
Matawan
(732) 583-3433

Smoker's Haven
470 Main St.
Metuchen
(732) 321-1442

Vans Smoke Shop
102 S. Main St.
Milltown
(732) 246-8292

Neptune Smoke Shop
706 State Route 35
Neptune
(732) 774-7373

Tinder Box
65 Church St.
New Brunswick
(732) 418-9896

Your Coffee & Cigar Box
703 Tilton Rd.
Northfield
(609) 645-0051

Tobacco Barn
1256 Stelton Rd.
Piscataway
(732) 572-7855

A Little Taste of Cuba
70 Witherspoon St.
Princeton
(609) 683-8988

Windsor Cigar Co.
33 Princeton Hightstown
   Rd. #L
Princeton Jct.
(609) 936-0600

Ashes Cigar Club
33 Broad St.
Red Bank
(732) 219-0710

Cigars Plus
68 White St.
Red Bank
(732) 212-9888

Tobacco Shop
10 Chestnut St.
Ridgewood
(201) 447-2204

Greentree Tobacco Co.
137 Egg Harbor Rd.
Sewell
(856) 374-4010

Cigar Stop
1067 Broad St.
Shrewsbury
(732) 460-0100

Don Francisco Cigars
295 New Brunswick Ave.
Spotswood
(732) 432-4099

Boulevard Cigar Shop
638 Fischer Blvd.
Toms River
(732) 288-2744

Di Franco's Pipe & Tobacco
797 Hwy. 33
Trenton
(609) 587-6375

Williams Totally Tobacco
137 S. Delsea Dr.
Vineland
(856) 692-8034

J•R Cigar
301 Route 10 E.
Whippany
(973) 887-0800

NEW MEXICO

Shelley's Smoke Shop
210 N. White Sands Blvd.
Alamogordo
(575) 443-0291

Bien Mur Travel Center Smoke
   Shop
100 Bien Mur Dr. N.E.
Albuquerque
(505) 821-5400

Duke City Cigars
7600 Jefferson St. N.E.
Albuquerque
(505) 797-9688

Full Spectrum
5300 Sequoia Rd. N.W.
Albuquerque
(505) 836-4909

Hookah Kings
4014 Central Ave. S.E.
Albuquerque
(505) 242-3907

Jack's Smoke Shop
518 Central Ave. S.W.
Albuquerque
(505) 242-6705

M&M Smoke Shop
1800 Central Ave. S.E.
Albuquerque
(505) 508-2035

Mike Smoke Shop
1701 Eubank Blvd. N.E.
Albuquerque
(505) 463-0584

Monte's Fine Cigars
3636 San Mateo Blvd. N.E.
Albuquerque
(505) 881-7999

Pajarito Store
5940 Isleta Blvd. S.W.
Albuquerque
(505) 873-7848

Pueblo Smoke Shop
2401 12th St. N.W.
Albuquerque
(505) 843-7270

Ray One Smoke Shop
825 Coors Blvd. N.W.
Albuquerque
(505) 255-0344

Ray's Smoke Shop
1300 Juan Tabo Blvd. N.E.
Albuquerque
(505) 299-6626

Ricky's Smoke Shop
204 Wyoming Blvd. S.E.
Albuquerque
(505) 268-5680

Stag Tobacconist
11200 Montgomery Blvd. N.E.
Albuquerque
(505) 237-9366

Tiwa 66
1660 Roy Ave.
Albuquerque
(505) 897-1701

Tobacco Road
902 Juan Tabo Blvd. N.E.
Albuquerque
(505) 237-2002

Tobacco Road
5350 Academy Rd. N.E.
Albuquerque
(505) 821-5074

Up in Smoke
5921 4th St. N.W.
Albuquerque
(505) 345-1196

Leno's Smoke Shop
3741 State Hwy. 47
Bosque Farms
(505) 869-3890

Silver Feather Gallery & Smoke
3508 State Hwy. 47
Bosque Farms
(505) 869-3317

Cohiba Smoke Shop
1604 E. Historic Hwy. 66
Gallup
(505) 863-6843

Santa Fe Smoke Shop
211 W. Santa Fe Ave.
Grants
(505) 287-9855

Lucas Pipe & Tobacco
201 E. University Ave.
Las Cruces
(575) 526-3411

Smokin Two
1940 S. Espina St.
Las Cruces
(575) 647-1682

C J's Smoke Shop
508 Historic US 66
Moriarty
(505) 832-1518

Picuris Pueblo Smoke Shop
1378 New Mexico 75
Penasco
(575) 587-2374

K C Express
601 W. 2nd St.
Portales
(575) 356-3129

Rio Rancho Cigars
1520 Deborah Rd. S.E.
Rio Rancho
(505) 994-9898

Noisy River Cigar Lounge
2629 Sudderth Dr.
Ruidoso
(575) 446-4884

Concrete Jungle Smoke Shop
126 N. Guadalupe St.
Santa Fe
(505) 820-2888

Dio Gene's Cigar Club
1413 Paseo De Peralta
Santa Fe
(505) 986-8251

Santa Fe Cigar Co.
510 Galisteo St.
Santa Fe
(505) 982-1044

Stag Tobacconist
947 W. Alameda St.
Santa Fe
(505) 982-3242

Smoke Shop
1408 N. Hudson St.
Silver City
(575) 388-5575

NEW YORK

Jan's Smoke & Craft Shop
383 Bloomingdale Rd.
Akron
(716) 542-4006

Edleez Tobacco Inc.
1475 Western Ave. # 8
Albany
(518) 489-6872

Habana Premium Cigar
   Shoppe
1537 Central Ave.
Albany
(518) 690-2222

Habana Premium Cigar
   Shoppe
8 Petra Lane
Albany
(518) 690-1293

Smoker Ltd.
810 Cortland St.
Albany
(518) 462-1302

Smokers Paradise Store
90 State St.
Albany
(518) 463-9838

Village Tobacconist
76 Deer Park Ave.
Babylon
(631) 661-8406

One Stop Smoke Shop
985 Atlantic Ave.
Baldwin
(516) 377-3855

Parth Smoke Shop
45 E. Genesee St.
Baldwinsville
(315) 635-3320

Arrowhawk Smoke Shop
852 Bloomingdale Rd.
Basom
(716) 542-6212

Rez Smoke & Craft Shop
986 Bloomingdale Rd.
Basom
(716) 542-2887

Go Ask Alice
73 Main St.
Brockport
(585) 637-8080

Arthur Avenue Cigars & Lounge
2332 Arthur Ave.
Bronx
(646) 393-5202

Country Club Cigars
3838 E. Tremont Ave.
Bronx
(718) 975-4501

La Casa Grande
2344 Arthur Ave.
Bronx
(718) 364-4657

Smoke Shop
265 E. 167th St.
Bronx
(718) 538-0177

A & M Optimo
439 5th Ave.
Brooklyn
(718) 788-7511

Arcade Cigar Store
460 4th Ave.
Brooklyn
(718) 788-0300

Barney's Smoke Shop
60 Schermerhorn St.
Brooklyn
(718) 875-8355

Cigar Imporium
1953 86th St.
Brooklyn
(718) 714-9289

Cigar Vault
1701 Ave. Z
Brooklyn
(718) 332-5534

18th Ave Smoke Shop Discount
8120 18th Ave.
Brooklyn
(718) 621-2194

M & K Smoke Shop
583 Fulton St.
Brooklyn
(718) 935-0948

Nevins Smoke Shop
20 Nevins St.
Brooklyn
(718) 858-9056

Rada Smoke Shop
3817 Ave. L
Brooklyn
(718) 758-0204

Velvet Cigar Lounge
174 Broadway
Brooklyn
(718) 302-4427

Bellezia Tobacco Shop
4549 Main St.
Buffalo
(716) 839-5381

Tinder Box
8212 Transit Rd.
Buffalo
(716) 689-2914

Virgil Avenue Tobacconist
6 Virgil Ave.
Buffalo
(716) 873-6461

All Mixed Up
8140 Brewerton Rd.
Cicero
(315) 698-4330

Park-Lane Tobacconist
15 Park Ave.
Clifton Park
(518) 371-6274

Happy Smoke Shop
473 Grand Blvd.
Deer Park
(631) 940-5041

Friar Tuck Bookshop and
    Tobacconist
180 Delaware Ave.
Delmar
(518) 439-3742

Nice Ash Cigars & Lounge
5334 Transit Rd.
Depew
(716) 685-7970

East End Cigar Co.
246 Larkfield Rd.
East Northport
(631) 754-6639

Zonen Limited
6697 Old Collamer Rd.
East Syracuse
(315) 437-3000

Smoking Cigars LLC
116 S. Central Ave.
Elmsford
(914) 592-1580

Edward Thomas Cigar
104 Limestone Plaza
Fayetteville
(315) 637-1688

Franklin Smoke Shop
774 Hempstead Turnpike
Franklin Square
(516) 216-1220

Maxis Cigar Shop
749 Hempstead Turnpike
Franklin Square
(516) 505-1489

Baroody's Cigar Store
405 Exchange St.
Geneva
(315) 789-3183

Maxis Smoke Shop
25314 Union Turnpike
Glen Oaks
(718) 343-5000

S T Smoke Shop
14195 New York 438
Gowanda
(716) 532-0843

Tobacco Plaza Ltd.
218 Lakeville Rd.
Great Neck
(516) 829-7134

Fat Jakes Cigar Palor
14 S. Buffalo St.
Hamburg
(716) 646-6336

Tobacco Corner
117 Walt Whitman Rd.
Huntington Station
(631) 425-7665

Trade Winds Cigar LLC
454 Main St.
Islip
(631) 277-6088

C & C Tobacco
109 N. Meadow St.
Ithaca
(607) 272-0637

State Smoke Shop
124 W. State St.
Ithaca
(607) 273-4270

Uptown Cigar Co.
32 John St.
Kingston
(845) 340-1142

J & K Smoke Shop
3201 Middle Country Rd.
Lake Grove
(631) 737-9297

Duke Bazzel Tobacco & Lounge
579 Troy Schenectady Rd.
Latham
(518) 785-0966

Smokers Choice
671 New Loudon Rd.
Latham
(518) 782-9365

Nicks Smoke Shop
170 N. Wellwood Ave.
Lindenhurst
(631) 956-3669

Kieffer's Cigar Store
409 Tulip St.
Liverpool
(315) 701-2444

Smitty's Smoke Shop
7537 S. State St.
Lowville
(315) 376-8173

Joannes Smoke Shop
1484 Montauk Hwy.
Mastic
(631) 395-4618

Little Rose Smoke Shop
128 Poospatuck Lane
Mastic
(631) 772-1190

Moniques Smoke Shop
108A Poospatuck Lane
Mastic
(631) 874-3008

Peace Pipe Smoke Shop
9 Squaw Lane
Mastic
(631) 395-4821

Red Dot Feather Smoke Shop
115 Poospatuck Lane
Mastic
(631) 878-2975

Smoke Signal Smoke Shop
134 Poospatuck Lane
Mastic
(631) 281-7193

Smoking Arrow Smokes
159 Poospatuck Lane
Mastic
(631) 281-1982

Fortune Smoke World
1701 E. Merrick Rd.
Merrick
(516) 868-2342

Smokers Gift Harbor
29 E. Main St.
Mt. Kisco
(914) 666-2648

Jim's Smoke Shop II
331 Route 25A
Mt. Sinai
(631) 331-4370

Village Sensations
111 Main St. #A
Nanuet
(845) 623-2222

Onondaga Nation Smoke Shop
Old Route 11
Nedrow
(315) 469-6932

Hudson Valley Cigars
475 Temple Hill Rd.
New Windsor
(845) 562-1762

Amazing Store & Smoke Shop
208 Columbus Ave.
New York
(212) 501-0400

Asia Enterprise Smoke Shop
1790 Broadway
New York
(212) 582-4116

B & K Smoke Shop
110 Maiden Lane
New York
(212) 425-5033

Barclay-Rex
570 Lexington Ave.
New York
(212) 888-1015

Barclay-Rex Pipe Shop
75 Broad St.
New York
(212) 809-4394

Barclay-Rex Pipe Shop
70 E. 42nd St.
New York
(212) 692-9680

Best Cigar Imports Inc.
21 Spring St.
New York
(212) 966-4233

Chavgan Cigar Store
137 E. 56th St.
New York
(212) 759-0317

Cigar Inn
1314 1st Ave.
New York
(212) 717-7403

Cigar Inn
1016 2nd Ave.
New York
(212) 750-0809

Cigar Landing Inc.
1585 Broadway
New York
(212) 489-2239

Cigar Smoke Shop
110 7th Ave. S.
New York
(212) 242-3872

Cigarillos Inc.
191 Spring St.
New York
(212) 334-2250

Classic Smoke Shop
206 Thompson St.
New York
(212) 777-9272

Club Macanudo Inc.
26 E. 63rd St.
New York
(212) 752-8200

Corner Smoke Shop
851 2nd Ave.
New York
(212) 867-0950

D P Cigars Corporation
265 W. 30th St.
New York
(212) 367-8949

Das Smoke Shop
26 Broadway
New York
(212) 747-0314

Davidoff At Columbus Circle
10 Columbus Circle
New York
(212) 823-6383

Davidoff of Geneva
535 Madison Ave.
New York
(212) 751-9060

De La Concha Tobacconist Inc.
1390 Ave. of the Americas
New York
(212) 757-3167

Famous Smoke Shop
55 W. 39th St.
New York
(212) 840-4093

First Avenue Smoke Shop
1666 1st Ave.
New York
(646) 672-9310

Grand Havana Room New
   York Inc.
666 5th Ave.
New York
(212) 245-1600

H & V Smoke Shop
39 W. 32nd St.
New York
(212) 868-5889

International Smoke Shop
809 8th Ave.
New York
(646) 557-0501

Jonil Smoke Shop Inc.
245 3rd Ave.
New York
(212) 982-0420

La Rosa Cubana Hand Made
   Cigar
862 Ave. of the Americas #2
New York
(212) 532-7450

Lafayette Smoke Shop Inc.
63 Spring St.
New York
(212) 226-3475

Madison Cigar Lounge (MCL)
1825 Madison Ave.
New York
(212) 348-7028

Martinez Handmade Cigars
171 W. 29th St.
New York
(212) 239-4049

Members' Smoke Shop
18 Broad St.
New York
(212) 344-5886

MidTown Cigar
562 5th Ave.
New York
(212) 997-2227

Mulberry Street Cigar Co.
140 Mulberry St.
New York
(212) 941-7400

Nat Sherman International
12 E. 42nd St.
New York
(212) 764-5000

O K Cigars
383 W. Broadway
New York
(212) 965-9065

Portes Cigar
5009 Broadway
New York
(212) 544-9623

S & L Smoke Shop
182 Broadway
New York
(212) 349-2219

Scottie's Smoke Shop
2 Lafayette St.
New York
(212) 964-8779

Smoke Scene
845 7th Ave.
New York
(212) 265-1425

Smoking Stop
45 Christopher St.
New York
(212) 929-1151

Taino Cigar
506 9th Ave.
New York
(212) 714-0858

Three Little Indians Cigar Co.
192 Grand St.
New York
(212) 334-5839

Baldwin Smoke Shop
1757 Grand Ave.
North Baldwin
(516) 223-9739

Nyack Tobacco Co. Inc.
140 Main St.
Nyack
(845) 358-9300

Tobacco Connection
3224 Long Beach Rd.
Oceanside
(516) 763-4300

Jim's Smoke Shop
582 S. Service Rd.
Patchogue
(631) 289-6405

The Burning Leaf Tobacco
  Shoppe
53 Clinton St.
Plattsburgh
(518) 562-3124

Smoke Signals
308 Main St.
Port Jefferson
(631) 928-3060

Cup O' Joes
959 State Route 9
Queensbury
(518) 615-0107

Rhinebeck Smoke Shop
2 E. Market St.
Rhinebeck
(845) 876-7185

Myrtle Avenue Shop Inc.
5402 Myrtle Ave.
Ridgewood
(718) 497-8087

North Fork Tobacco
487 Main Rd.
Riverhead
(631) 722-2660

Cigar Factory
467 State St.
Rochester
(585) 325-7220

Dewey Avenue Smoke Shop
1405 Dewey Ave.
Rochester
(585) 458-8824

Elab Boutique
719 Monroe Ave.
Rochester
(585) 473-5882

Elab Boutique
4373 Lake Ave.
Rochester
(585) 865-4513

Havana House
365 N. Washington St.
Rochester
(585) 586-0620

Havana Moe's Cigars
125 E. Ave.
Rochester
(585) 325-1030

Look Ah Hookah
1635 E. Henrietta Rd.
Rochester
(585) 292-5665

OJ's Smoke Shop
504 S. James St.
Rome
(315) 337-0526

Cioffis Cigars
215 Ronkonkoma Ave.
Ronkonkoma
(631) 467-8473

Matador Cigars
38 Lincoln Ave.
Roslyn Heights
(516) 626-4966

Cigar Bar, The
2 Main St.
Sag Harbor
(631) 725-2575

James and Sons Tobacconists
360 Broadway
Saratoga Springs
(518) 581-7274

Smokin' Sam's Cigar Shop
5 Caroline St.
Saratoga Springs
(518) 587-6450

Tobacco Outfitters
69 Partition St.
Saugerties
(845) 246-8424

Mom's Cigars
1119 Central Park Ave.
Scarsdale
(914) 723-3088

Gator's Cigar Shop
1550 Altamont Ave.
Schenectady
(518) 356-6805

Habana Premium Cigar
  Shoppe
180 Erie Blvd.
Schenectady
(518) 346-4052

Orion Boutique
169 Jay St.
Schenectady
(518) 346-4902

Doc James Cigars & Golf
3691 Old Yorktown Rd.
Shrub Oak
(914) 962-9388

Mr Tobacco
126 E. Main St.
Smithtown
(631) 724-7463

Shinnecock Smoke Shop
50 Montauk Hwy.
Southampton
(631) 287-9578

Carmine's Cigars
1671 Richmond Rd.
Staten Island
(718) 351-6637

Carmine's Cigars II
3872 Richmond Ave.
Staten Island
(718) 605-5801

Cigar Aficion
965 Richmond Ave.
Staten Island
(718) 761-1234

Empire Smoke Shop
1398 Forest Ave.
Staten Island
(718) 815-4444

Global Smoke Shop
600 Jericho Turnpike
Syosset
(516) 714-8005

Barbieri's Specialty Cigars
304 S. Main St.
Syracuse
(315) 458-8070

Chase's Cigar Store
2829 James St.
Syracuse
(315) 463-9334

Downtown Smoke Shop
359 S. Salina St.
Syracuse
(315) 475-0004

Jones McIntosh Tobacco
4036 New Court Ave.
Syracuse
(315) 463-9183

Mallard Tobacconist
208 Walton St.
Syracuse
(315) 475-5839

North Salina Cigar Store
851 N. Salina St.
Syracuse
(315) 475-3988

Smokers Choice
120 Hoosick St.
Troy
(518) 272-0398

J Q Cigar Hut
2022 Empire Blvd.
Webster
(585) 671-3170

Smoker's Haven of the
 Southtowns
1167 Union Rd.
West Seneca
(716) 675-6195

Fortune Smoke Shop
527 Old Country Rd.
Westbury
(516) 997-8109

A & N Tobacco Shop
125 Westchester Ave.
White Plains
(914) 946-2835

White Plains Disc Smoke Shop
12 Quarropas St.
White Plains
(914) 946-2996

Hillside Cigar Shop
338 Hillside Ave.
Williston Park
(516) 873-7905

Harry's Cigars
650 Central Park Ave.
Yonkers
(914) 751-7161

NORTH CAROLINA
Octopus Garden Smoke Shop
140 Airport Rd., Ste. M
Arden
(828) 654-0906

Antique Tobacco Barn
75 Swannanoa River Rd.
Asheville
(828) 252-7291

B & B Tobacconists
377 Merrimon Ave.
Asheville
(828) 253-8822

Carolina Cigar Co.
45 Broadway St.
Asheville
(828) 281-1500

Octopus Garden II
1062 Patton Ave.
Asheville
(828) 232-6030

Pipes Limited
3 S. Tunnel Rd.
Asheville
(828) 298-2392

Tobacco Jr
2589 Eric Lane
Burlington
(336) 222-1261

Tobacco Store
126 N. Sellars Mill Rd.
Burlington
(336) 226-4051

Calabash Smoke Shop
9970 Beach Dr. S.W.
Calabash
(910) 575-7667

Tar Heel Tobacco
104 NC 54, #CC
Carrboro
(919) 969-8777

K & S Cigars
750 E. Chatham St.
Cary
(919) 467-3235

Tobacconists of Cary
2434 S.W. Cary Pkwy.
Cary
(919) 469-4262

Charlotte Cigar & Collectibles
4300 Sharon Rd.
Charlotte
(704) 364-2990

Cigars Central Inc.
3712 E. Independence Blvd.
Charlotte
(704) 566-6063

Cigars Etc. 2
1636 Sardis Rd. N.
Charlotte
(704) 532-9853

Cutters
100 W. Trade St.
Charlotte
(704) 358-6556

Infinity's End
5119 S. Blvd.
Charlotte
(704) 369-0223

Infinity's End
5722 E. Independence Blvd.
Charlotte
(704) 536-7451

Mc Cranie's
4143 Park Rd.
Charlotte
(704) 523-8554

One Stop Smoke Shop
9630 University City Blvd.
Charlotte
(704) 548-9190

Outland Cigar Club
14815 John J Delaney Dr.
Charlotte
(704) 369-5500

Penguins
2133 Southend Dr.
Charlotte
(704) 807-5853

Smokers Depot
3039 S. Blvd.
Charlotte
(704) 527-4377

Smokers Depot
9640 S. Tryon St.
Charlotte
(704) 504-9220

Sunshine Daydreams
3225 N. Davidson St.
Charlotte
(704) 332-4367

Tinder Box
200 S. College St.
Charlotte
(704) 334-3449

Tinder Box
7852 Rea Rd.
Charlotte
(704) 541-0034

Tinderbox
4440 Sharon Rd.
Charlotte
(704) 366-5492

Tobacco Trader
8152 South Tryon St., Unit D
Charlotte
(704) 588-0440

Tobacco House
100 W. Church St.
Cherryville
(704) 435-1190

McCranie's
20910 Torrence Chapel Rd.
Cornelius
(704) 655-9055

Tinder Box
6910 Fayetteville Rd.
Durham
(919) 806-5533

A Mart Tobacco Shop
6460 Yadkin Rd.
Fayetteville
(910) 864-0502

Cliffdale Mart & Tobacco
8200 Cliffdale Rd.
Fayetteville
(910) 864-8152

Golden Tobacco & Cigar
4537 Raeford Rd.
Fayetteville
(910) 486-0900

Highlander Cigar Co.
308 Hay St.
Fayetteville
(910) 323-0440

It'z Cigar Parlor
4118 Legend Ave.
Fayetteville
(910) 826-2305

R J Tobacco Mart
407 Hope Mills Rd.
Fayetteville
(919) 598-9683

Smoke Shop
5701 Yadkin Rd.
Fayetteville
(910) 867-9770

Tobacco Center
7707 S. Raeford Rd.
Fayetteville
(910) 860-1500

Tobacco Mart
1940 Skibo Rd.
Fayetteville
(910) 860-4824

Westwood Tobacco Shop
434 Westwood Shopping
  Center
Fayetteville
(910) 487-8600

Boutique Hypnotica
908 Spring Garden St.
Greensboro
(336) 333-2346

Cheap Smokes & Cigars
3739 High Point Rd.
Greensboro
(336) 297-9797

Lorillard Tobacco Co.
714 Green Valley Rd.
Greensboro
(336) 335-1060

Pipe and Pint, The
2500 Spring Garden St.
Greensboro
(336) 218-8610

Tobacco Shop
3719 Farmington Dr.
Greensboro
(336) 851-0150

Expressions
424 Evans St.
Greenville
(252) 758-6685

Fatty's Tobacco & Trinkets
505 Evans St.
Greenville
(252) 561-8796

Sir Toms Tobacco Emporium
129 4th Ave. W.
Hendersonville
(828) 697-7753

Pipes Ltd.
174 Valley Rd.
Hickory
(828) 328-8002

Outman Knife & Cigar
Cranlyn Rd.
Huntersville
(704) 892-5112

Northwood Tobacco Shop
334 Henderson Dr.
Jacksonville
(910) 455-0629

Tobacco Country USA
461 Western Blvd.
Jacksonville
(910) 353-6115

Triad Smoke Shop LLC
202 W. Mountain St.
Kernersville
(336) 992-4500

TNT Smoke Shop
1975 Cotton Grove Rd.
Lexington
(336) 357-0573

Smoker's Edge
4314 Wilkinson Blvd.
Lowell
(704) 823-0170

Churchill's Cigars Tobacco
and Gifts
5087 US 70
Morehead City
(252) 727-1993

Tobacco Shop & Gifts
1250 US Hwy. 70 E.
New Bern
(252) 636-5900

Buddha's Belly
2112 Hillsborough St.
Raleigh
(919) 664-8099

Empire Cigars
9650 Strickland Rd.
Raleigh
(919) 870-0081

Pipes By George
1209 Hillsborough St.
Raleigh
(919) 829-1167

Royal Blunts Connections
4900 Thornton Rd.
Raleigh
(919) 790-8139

Smoker Friendly
1436 Garner Station Blvd.
Raleigh
(919) 662-9935

Smoker Friendly
6300 Creedmoor Rd.
Raleigh
(919) 866-9002

Tinder Box
4325 Glenwood Ave.
Raleigh
(919) 787-1310

Tobacco & Gifts
3281 Avent Ferry Rd.
Raleigh
(919) 854-1988

D & R Tobacco
211 Mallard Rd.
Smithfield
(919) 989-9458

Tobacco Shop & Gift
1169 N. Bragg Blvd.
Spring Lake
(910) 496-0121

Jr Tobacco of America Inc.
1515 E. Broad St.
Statesville
(800) 577-6653

Carolina Cigar Co.
414 W. Main St.
Sylva
(828) 631-2328

Brooklynn Cigars
7134 Market St.
Wilmington
(910) 686-2446

Carolina Tobacco Shop
2841 Carolina Beach Rd.
Wilmington
(910) 794-7033

Cigar Exchange
107 Market St.
Wilmington
(910) 251-5015

Davis & Son Tobacconists Inc.
3807 Oleander Dr.
Wilmington
(910) 791-6688

Expressions In Wilmington
419 S College Rd.
Wilmington
(910) 793-0203

East Carolina Ryo LLC
1920 Farrior St.
Wilson
(252) 291-0006

Smokers Choice Tobacco Outlet
2200 US Hwy. 301 S.
Wilson
(252) 243-2131

Smokers Palace
4916 Hayes Place
Wilson
(252) 237-9912

Circle C Mart & Smoke Shop
2618 Hickory Tree Rd.
Winston Salem
(336) 764-5750

R J Reynolds Tobacco Co.
401 N. Main St.
Winston Salem
(336) 983-1200

Robinhood Tobacco
3443 Robinhood Rd.
Winston Salem
(336) 774-8000

Smoke Shop
11141 Old US Hwy. 52
Winston Salem
(336) 764-0707

Tinder Box
3320 Silas Creek Pkwy. S.W.
Winston Salem
(336) 765-5165

NORTH DAKOTA
Frank Mc Kone Cigar Co.
742 19th St. N.
Fargo
(701) 235-4261

Woodchuck, The
1418 1st Ave. N.
Fargo
(701) 232-6876

Smoke Signs
108 Main Ave. N.
Hankinson
(701) 242-7100

OHIO
Lakes Discount
852 Portage Lakes Dr.
Akron
(330) 644-0720

Smokers' Choice
382 E. Waterloo Rd.
Akron
(330) 785-1235

Smoker's Den
1288 E. Tallmadge Ave.
Akron
(330) 633-3141

Smokers Outlet Store
508 Canton Rd.
Akron
(330) 794-2233

Smoker's World Inc.
1712 W. Market St.
Akron
(330) 864-3800

Cousin's Cigar
36050 Detroit Rd.
Avon
(440) 934-9909

Wharf, The
3464 New German Trebien Rd.
Beavercreek
(937) 426-0633

Butt's
402 E. Wooster St.
Bowling Green
(419) 352-2888

Briarpatch
2880 Whipple Ave. N.W.
Canton
(330) 477-2511

Osi Tobacco
3915 Everhard Rd. N.W.
Canton
(330) 494-6152

Mac's Tobacco Pouch
48 Shopping Plaza
Chagrin Falls
(440) 247-5365

Bell's House of Tobacco
12137 Royal Point Dr.
Cincinnati
(513) 774-0270

Choice Cigars & Tobacco
545 Clough Pike
Cincinnati
(513) 528-6160

Cinti Tobacconist
617 Vine St.
Cincinnati
(513) 621-9932

House of Smokes
11259 Reading Rd.
Cincinnati
(513) 769-1608

Smoke Store
2824 Jefferson Ave.
Cincinnati
(513) 569-0420

Straus Tobacconist
410 Walnut St.
Cincinnati
(513) 621-3388

Cigar Cigars
21808 Center Ridge Rd.
Cleveland
(440) 333-5454

Cousin's Cigar Co.
28400 Chagrin Blvd.
Cleveland
(216) 464-9396

Cousins Cigars
1828 Euclid Ave.
Cleveland
(216) 781-9390

Dad's Smoke Shop
17112 Lorain Ave.
Cleveland
(216) 671-3663

Holy Smokes
7872 Broadview Rd.
Cleveland
(216) 520-6995

Jovann's Tobacco Shop
6260 Mayfield Rd.
Cleveland
(440) 442-4775

Mayfield Smoke Shop
12307 Mayfield Rd.
Cleveland
(216) 229-1588

Parma Heights Smoke Shop
6647 Pearl Rd.
Cleveland
(440) 886-3449

Port Royal Cigar
33540 Aurora Rd.
Cleveland
(440) 914-0500

Sam Klein Cigar Co.
1834 E. 6th St.
Cleveland
(216) 621-2673

Smoke Zone II
13034 Lorain Ave.
Cleveland
(216) 251-3425

Tobacco Co.
6493 Pearl Rd.
Cleveland
(440) 842-1988

Barclay Pipe & Tobacco
1677 W. Lane Ave.
Columbus
(614) 486-4243

Barclay Tobacco & Cigar
2673 Federated Blvd.
Columbus
(614) 764-0300

Burning Leaf Cigars
1044 S. High St.
Columbus
(614) 443-5323

Dream Merchant
17 E. 13th Ave.
Columbus
(614) 586-1589

New Havana Cigars LLC
1183 Chesapeake Ave.
Columbus
(614) 486-2822

Puff N Stuff
1652 N. High St.
Columbus
(614) 298-7883

Smoke Signals
8657 Sancus Blvd.
Columbus
(614) 436-0595

Smoker's Haven
2477 N. High St.
Columbus
(614) 299-2442

Twisted Vine, The
1816 W. 5th Ave.
Columbus
(614) 488-6113

Tinder Box at Easton
4028 Townsfair Way
Columbus
(614) 475-7872

Tobacco International
18 E. 13th Ave.
Columbus
(614) 291-3484

Arrow Wine Smoke Shop
615 Lyons Rd.
Dayton
(937) 433-6778

Boston Stoker
6071 Far Hills Ave.
Dayton
(937) 439-2400

Miami Cigar & Tobacco Co.
1876 Radio Rd.
Dayton
(937) 252-9901

Speedway
2050 E. Stroop Rd.
Dayton
(937) 395-3617

Tobacco Shack
5200 Markey Rd.
Dayton
(937) 275-7030

Woodland Cigar Co. LLC
46 N. Sandusky St.
Delaware
(740) 368-8572

Electro Smoke Inc.
5043 Tuttle Crossing Blvd.
Dublin
(614) 336-8159

Tinder Box
5911 Karric Square Dr.
Dublin
(614) 761-3120

Smoker's Outlet
586 Cleveland St.
Elyria
(440) 365-7133

CR Butts Discount Tobacco
606 Taywood Rd.
Englewood
(937) 832-4880

Smoke Shop
1060 E. 2nd St.
Franklin
(937) 704-0218

Hey Have A Cigar Co.
1151 N. Hamilton Rd.
Gahanna
(614) 478-1000

Royal Tobacco and Cigars
4700 Cemetery Rd.
Hilliard
(614) 777-1227

Midnight Oasis
1108 S. Water St.
Kent
(330) 677-8011

Emporium-Downtown
207 W. Main St.
Lancaster
(740) 653-5717

Exquisite Tobacco
1020 W. Fair Ave.
Lancaster
(740) 653-6330

Rags 2 Riches
936 Broadway
Lorain
(440) 245-7247

City News—Suzy's Smoke
   Room
100 N. Main St.
Mansfield
(419) 524-0261

Puffs Cigarette & Tobacco
840 N. Trimble Rd.
Mansfield
(419) 747-6667

United Smokes of America
717 Delaware Ave.
Marion
(740) 387-2745

Cigar Affair, The
323 Conant St.
Maumee
(419) 891-0109

Bullocks Smoke Shop
400 Vernonview Dr.
Mt. Vernon
(740) 397-7978

Humidor
267 Deo Dr.
Newark
(740) 366-1881

Knobby's Shop
333 N. Main St.
Piqua
(937) 773-0081

Mickey's Smoke Shop
1308 E. Perry St.
Port Clinton
(419) 734-5889

Shawnee Cigar Co.
9226 Dublin Rd.
Powell
(614) 791-9210

Timba Cigar Co.
162 W. Olentangy St.
Powell
(614) 760-9730

Butt Hut
6172 N. Summit St.
Toledo
(419) 729-2888

Cigar Merchant
1415 W. Sylvania Ave.
Toledo
(419) 478-6747

Smoke Shack
5235 Dorr St.
Toledo
(419) 578-2924

M J Mugsy's
123 W. Wyandot Ave.
Upper Sandusky
(419) 294-5355

Tobacco Man
5992 Westerville Rd.
Westerville
(614) 895-1325

Uptown Cigar Co.
33 N. State St.
Westerville
(614) 392-2302

OKLAHOMA

Sports Zone
56371 E. Hwy. 125
Afton
(918) 257-5357

J J's Smoke Shop
702 E. Central Blvd.
Anadarko
(405) 247-9690

Beeline Smoke Shop Inc.
4985 Hwy. 75
Beggs
(918) 267-4700

3 Elks Smoke Shop
620 B Ave.
Bixby
(918) 366-6160

Monarch Pipe Co.
115 E. 2nd Ave.
Bristow
(918) 367-3217

Smoke Shop 66
Hwy. 66 W.
Chandler
(405) 258-1260

Crossroads Smoke Shop
10567 Meers Porter Hill Rd.
Elgin
(580) 492-6886

Emilio's Piano Lounge
221 W. Randolph Ave.
Enid
(580) 234-5525

NID Smoke Shop
221 E. Own K Garriott Rd.
Enid
(580) 233-6311

Pete's Smoke Shop
508 N. 30th St.
Enid
(580) 234-5487

Smoke Signal No. 109
432 S. Van Buren St.
Enid
(580) 233-6561

Beans and Briar
620 SW. Centre Ave.
Lawton
(580) 357-2830

Lee Boulevard Smoke Shop
1502 SE. Lee Blvd.
Lawton
(580) 353-4110

Railroad Smokeshop
2202 S. Railroad
Lawton
(580) 248-0083

North Main Smoke Shop
720 N. Main St.
McAlester
(918) 423-5930

Plantations
3207 W. Main St.
Norman
(405) 364-5152

Royal Pipes and Tobacco
Limited
105 E. Boyd St.
Norman
(405) 364-5151

C and C Tobacco
1150 NE. 36th St.
Oklahoma City
(405) 424-4000

Cigar and Company Tobacco
Room
7101 N. May Ave.
Oklahoma City
(405) 843-1010

Drew's Tobacco World
4120 N. Portland Ave.
Oklahoma City
(405) 943-2876

Drew's Tobacco World
1514 SE. 44th St., Ste. D
Oklahoma City
(405) 677-7473

Outter Limits
7902 N. MacArthur Blvd.
Oklahoma City
(405) 720-7138

Pipe Dreamz
107 S. Sooner Rd.
Oklahoma City
(405) 702-9062

Smoken Okies
1111 N. Meridian Ave.
Oklahoma City
(405) 943-3737

Classic Cigars
8703 N. Owasso Expy., #0
Owasso
(918) 274-8191

Columbian Breeze
125 W. Joy Ave.
Pauls Valley
(405) 238-4680

82 Smoke Shop
Hwy. 82
Peggs
(918) 598-3046

Prague Smoke Shop
700 N. Jim Thorpe Blvd.
Prague
(405) 567-8008

Randlett Smoke Shop
Hwy. 70
Randlett
(580) 281-3855

Iron Post
Redwood St. and Central Rd.
Sallisaw
(918) 775-8430

Menagerie
200 N. Garfield Ave.
Sand Springs
(918) 245-5257

Independence Tobacco Shop
905 E. Independence St.
Shawnee
(405) 273-1221

169 Smoke Shop
Hwy. 169 N.
Talala
(918) 275-4332

Archers Tobacco Pouch Inc.
5976 S. Yale Ave.
Tulsa
(918) 742-1660

Firewalker Smoke Shop
1443 N. Rosedale Ave.
Tulsa
(918) 592-6722

Fogue and Bates Cigars
6929 E. 71st St.
Tulsa
(918) 488-0818

Independence Smoke Shop Inc.
743 N. Lewis Pl.
Tulsa
(918) 838-1106

North Lewis Smoke Shop
4343 N. Lewis Ave.
Tulsa
(918) 425-8446

Northridge Smoke Shop
5005 N. Peoria Ave.
Tulsa
(918) 430-1101

Papa Bears Smoke Shop
11690 E. 21st St.
Tulsa
(918) 437-8833

South Yale Smoke Shop
10940 S. Yale Ave.
Tulsa
(918) 298-1530

Pipestone Tobacco
433661 E. Hwy. 66
Vinita
(918) 323-0333

OREGON

Pipeline
2110 Pacific Blvd. S.W.
Albany
(541) 981-2364

TD Tobacco and Cigars
920 S.E. Clay St.
Albany
(541) 791-8419

Ashland Wine Cellar—
    Humidified Cigars
38 Lithia Way
Ashland
(541) 488-2111

Hot Box
4589 S.W. Watson Ave.
Beaverton
(503) 574-4057

Paul's Tobacco World
10425 S.W. Beaverton-
    Hillsdale Hwy.
Beaverton
(503) 626-3773

Timber Valley Tobaccos
12745 S.W. Walker Rd.
Beaverton
(503) 644-3837

Tony's Smoke Shop
12400 S.W. Broadway St.
Beaverton
(503) 597-0027

Cosmic Depot
342 N.E. Clay Ave.
Bend
(541) 385-7478

Specialty Cigars Int'l. Inc.
109 N.W. Greenwood Ave.
Bend
(541) 330-2486

Tony's Smoke Shop
1318 N.W. 9th St., Ste. B
Corvallis
(541) 753-0900

Briar Shoppe
278 Valley River Center
Eugene
(541) 343-4738

Hunky Dory Pipe & Tobacco
271 W. 7th Ave.
Eugene
(541) 345-1853

Legit Misfit, The
1680 W. 11th Ave.
Eugene
(541) 284-0420

Luckey's
933 Olive St.
Eugene
(541) 687-4643

Forest Grove Tobacco Shop
3034 Pacific Ave.
Forest Grove
(503) 359-9240

Cascade Cigar & Tobacco Co.
9691 S.E. 82nd Ave.
Happy Valley
(503) 775-5885

Five Friends
7432 W. Baseline Rd.
Hillsboro
(503) 649-2289

Rick's Smoke Shop
831 Main St.
Klamath Falls
(541) 884-0313

Rick's Smoke Shop
2209 Madison St.
Klamath Falls
(541) 884-0719

Rick's Smoke Shops
3009 Maywood Dr.
Klamath Falls
(541) 884-6951

E & L Tobacco Inc.
31054 Santiam Hwy.
Lebanon
(541) 258-8754

Tobacco Market
1695 S. Main St.
Lebanon
(541) 259-6168

U S Smoke Shop
1800 US 101
Lincoln City
(541) 996-4300

Gibb's Tobacco House
1220 N.E. Adams St.
McMinnville
(503) 434-6799

Happy Hut
343 N.E. Baker St.
McMinnville
(503) 435-1770

Victoria's Station
120 Galice Rd.
Merlin
(541) 471-1396

Astro
11010 S.E. McLoughlin Blvd.
Milwaukie
(503) 654-1066

Smokes & More
655 S. Main St.
Myrtle Creek
(541) 863-8823

Old School
281 S. Oregon St.
Ontario
(541) 823-0123

Astro
7510 N. Interstate Ave.
Portland
(503) 285-5308

Broadway Cigar Co.
3615 N.E. Broadway St.
Portland
(503) 473-8000

82nd Avenue Tobacco & Pipe
Ltd.
400 S.E. 82nd Ave.
Portland
(503) 255-9987

4th Avenue Smoke Shop &
Store
514 S.W. 4th Ave.
Portland
(503) 222-5236

Head East
13250 S.E. Division St.
Portland
(503) 761-3777

Jr's Smoke Shop
133 S.W. Broadway
Portland
(503) 278-3049

Nomad Crossing
3959 S.E. Hawthorne Blvd.
Portland
(503) 239-8009

Paul's Cigars
1523 N. Jantzen Ave.
Portland
(503) 283-4924

Pype's Palace
4760 N. Lombard St.
Portland
(503) 289-9298

Richie's Cigar Store
922 N.W. Flanders St.
Portland
(503) 595-5556

Rich's Cigar Store
820 S.W. Alder St.
Portland
(503) 228-1700

Rich's Cigar Store
706 N.W. 23rd Ave.
Portland
(503) 227-6907

Riverside Tobacco
2 S.W. 3rd Ave.
Portland
(971) 544-1200

Rose City Tobacco and Pipes
729 S.E. Morrison St.
Portland
(503) 232-2900

Smoke Signals on Sandy
3554 N.E. Sandy Blvd.
Portland
(503) 235-0504

Smokin'
8028 S.E. Powell Blvd.
Portland
(503) 772-0777

Still Smokin Tobacco for Less
12302 S.E. Powell Blvd.
Portland
(503) 762-4219

T J's Xpress
9320 N. Whitaker Rd.
Portland
(503) 286-9957

Tobacco 2 Go
4501 N.E. 138th Ave.
Portland
(503) 254-1810

Tobacco Town
4860 S.E. 82nd Ave.
Portland
(503) 771-7347

Tobacco Town Inc.
16575 S.E. McLoughlin Blvd.
Portland
(503) 656-4682

Up in Smoke
8213 N. Denver Ave.
Portland
(503) 735-3053

Boss Hoggs Smoke Shop
205 N.W. 3rd St.
Prineville
(541) 447-3672

Bridgeview Cigar & Tobacco
Shop
29375 Washington Way
Rainier
(503) 556-0151

Redmond Smoke & Gift
245 S.W. 6th St.
Redmond
(541) 923-6307

Tobacco Jo North
909 N.W. 6th St.
Redmond
(541) 923-2896

AVVA Cigars & Tobacco
831 Lancaster Dr. N.E.
Salem
(503) 585-5807

Habits
3345 Commercial St. S.E.
Salem
(503) 391-6028

Tobacco Pouch
1599 Edgewater St. N.W.
Salem
(503) 588-8060

Tobaccoville U S A
275 Lancaster Dr. S.E.
Salem
(503) 363-6574

Smoke Shoppe Etc.
125 W. Central Ave.
Sutherlin
(541) 459-4108

Tim's Great Cigars
23830 N.E. Halsey St.
Wood Village
(503) 665-2723

PENNSYLVANIA

Tobacco & Cigar Connoisseurs
4260 W. Tilghman St.
Allentown
(610) 530-7445

Monster Cigar Co.
2060 Street Rd.
Bensalem
(215) 639-5300

Cigars International
Superstore
4078 Nazareth Pike
Bethlehem
(484) 895-3933

Allegheny Smokeworks
217 Freeport Rd.
Blawnox
(412) 828-6653

Boswell's Pipe & Tobacco
586 Lincoln Way E.
Chambersburg
(717) 264-1711

Light'n Up Premier Smoke
Shop
130 W. Main St.
Collegeville
(610) 409-5630

Back Mountain Tobacco
324 Memorial Hwy.
Dallas
(570) 675-2663

Classic Cigar Parlor
12 N. Main St.
Doylestown
(215) 348-2880

Rock's Smoke Shop
7 Liberty Square
East Stroudsburg
(570) 223-6534

Famous Smoke Shop
1100 Conroy Place
Easton
(610) 559-8800

City Tobacco Co.
11 Gateway Shopping Center
Edwardsville
(570) 288-6585

Emmaus Smoke Shop
1245 Chestnut St., Unit A
Emmaus
(610) 965-3096

Frolic of Exton
325 E. Lincoln Hwy.
Exton
(610) 363-8890

J M Cigars
19 Marchwood Rd.
Exton
(610) 363-3063

Dave's Smoke Shop
509 Main St.
Forest City
(570) 785-2356

Light'n Up Premier Smoke Shop
480 Lancaster Ave.
Frazer
(610) 251-9117

Little Habana Cigar Shop
881 Eisenhower Blvd.
Harrisburg
(717) 939-3811

Rae's Tobacco
134 Strawberry St.
Harrisburg
(717) 233-1218

Wooden Indian Tobacco Shop
1305 W. Chester Pike
Havertown
(610) 449-7001

Cigar Box
218 Laurel Mall
Hazle Township
(570) 459-3099

Grand Smoke Shop
231 W. Mine St.
Hazleton
(570) 454-2202

Arrowhead Cigars
2511 Huntingdon Pike
Huntingdon Valley
(215) 947-7878

Olde World Tobacco
2213 Lincoln Hwy. E.
Lancaster
(717) 392-7830

Tinder Box
1623 Manheim Pike
Lancaster
(717) 560-4277

Tobacco Palace Inc.
219 Park City Center
Lancaster
(717) 397-7569

Tobacco Co.
829 State St.
Lemoyne
(717) 975-8877

Genuine Tobacco Co.
76 W. Frederick St.
Millersville
(717) 871-8431

A Little Taste of Cuba
102A S. Main St.
New Hope
(215) 862-1122

Ned's Cigar & Lottery Store
4 S. State St.
Newtown
(215) 968-6337

Up in Smoke Pipe Shop
601 W. Main St.
Palmyra
(717) 832-7700

Artifax
2446 Cottman Ave.
Philadelphia
(215) 331-0306

Avril 50
3406 Sansom St.
Philadelphia
(215) 222-6108

BNB Cigars
7920 Germantown Ave.
Philadelphia
(215) 242-6776

Chestnut Smoke & Gift Shop
87 S. 8th St.
Philadelphia
(215) 923-1699

Harry's Smoke Shop
14 N. 3rd St.
Philadelphia
(215) 925-4770

Holt's Cigar Co.
12270 Townsend Rd.
Philadelphia
(215) 676-3926

Holt's Cigar Co.
1522 Walnut St.
Philadelphia
(215) 732-8500

Liberty Smokes
2740 S. Front St.
Philadelphia
(215) 389-6001

Light'n Up Premier Smoke Shop
1100 S. Columbus Blvd.
Philadelphia
(215) 389-7911

Phil Herman's Cigar Store
1501 Walnut St.
Philadelphia
(215) 567-0144

Philadelphia Cigar & Tobacco
2417 Welsh Rd.
Philadelphia
(215) 464-2222

Philly Smoke Shop
2327 Cottman Ave.
Philadelphia
(215) 335-9878

S J Cigar Co.
524 S. 3rd St.
Philadelphia
(215) 440-0776

Tobacco Junction
9961 Bustleton Ave.
Philadelphia
(215) 464-2484

Twin Smoke Shoppe
1537 S. 10th St.
Philadelphia
(215) 334-0970

Wonderland
2037 Walnut St.
Philadelphia
(215) 561-1071

Bloom Cigar Co.
54 S. 12th St.
Pittsburgh
(412) 431-4277

Jernigan's Scotch & Cigar Bar
1500 Washington Rd., #1301
Pittsburgh
(412) 531-5881

Steamtown Cigar Club
407 Spruce St.
Scranton
(570) 344-1188

El Fumador Cigars & Pipes
518 Beaver St.
Sewickley
(412) 741-1300

Slippery Rock Cigars
278 Cameron Dr.
Slippery Rock
(724) 234-2439

Cigars Unlimited
1004 N. Bethlehem Pike
Spring House
(215) 643-2575

Your Cigar Den
127 S. Fraser St.
State College
(814) 867-0666

Stillwater Smokes Inc.
Maple Grove Rd.
Stillwater
(570) 925-2856

Atlantic Cigar Co.
600 Main St.
Stroudsburg
(570) 476-5730

Tobacco World
314 Morgantown St.
Uniontown
(724) 438-3534

Light'n Up Premier Smoke Shop
269 E. Swedesford Rd.
Wayne
(610) 687-3323

G & G Cigar Co.
118 N. High St.
West Chester
(610) 436-9999

El Humidor
525 Scott St.
Wilkes Barre
(570) 822-3544

Tobacco Center
21 W. Church St.
Williamsport
(570) 322-7766

Churchill Cigar Café
25 S. Main St.
Yardley
(215) 369-0966

RHODE ISLAND
Smoking Jacket
230 Waseca Ave.
Barrington
(401) 245-9393

Narragansett Indian Smoke
    Shop Annex
4477 S. County Trail
Charlestown
(401) 213-6180

Humidor Smoke Shop
1500 Oaklawn Ave.
Cranston
(401) 463-5949

Humidor Smoke Shop
5600 Post Rd.
East Greenwich
(401) 885-1285

Regency Cigar Emporium
752 Main St.
East Greenwich
(401) 884-7665

3 Amigos Cigar
752 Main St.
East Greenwich
(401) 885-4700

3 Guys Cigar Co.
79 Wildwood Trail
East Greenwich
(401) 886-5275

Cigar Box Ltd.
855 Point Judith Rd.
Narragansett
(401) 792-9309

Holy Smokes
9 Broadway
Newport
(401) 846-5948

Humidor Cigar World
182 Thames St.
Newport
(401) 842-0270

Tobacco Rd.
190 Admiral Kalbfus Rd.
Newport
(401) 619-1649

Ashes Cigar Lounge
1483 Mineral Spring Ave.
North Providence
(401) 649-4274

Jolly Roger's Smoke Shop
2009 Smith St.
North Providence
(888) 742-4427

Mr Cigar
1622 Mineral Spring Ave.
North Providence
(401) 353-5200

Smoke Stack Cigar Shop
2003 Smith St.
North Providence
(401) 349-0512

B K House of Cigars Inc.
530 Broadway
Pawtucket
(401) 726-1118

Habanos Cigar Lounge Inc.
424 Benefit St.
Pawtucket
(401) 729-5620

Cigar Masters
Westin Residences
1 W. Exchange St.
Providence
(401) 383-9002

Old World Cigar
345 Atwells Ave.
Providence
(401) 276-9150

Olde Smoke Shoppe
65 Weybosset St.
Providence
(401) 272-4699

Pippi's on the Hill LLC
136 Atwells Ave.
Providence
(401) 277-2800

Red Carpet Smoke Shop
108 Waterman St.
Providence
(401) 421-4499

Sir Winston's Tobacco
   Emporium
341 S. Main St.
Providence
(401) 861-5700

Smokeez Smoke Shop
21 Olneyville Square
Providence
(401) 421-1510

Zenobia
245 Meeting St.
Providence
(401) 680-7676

Smithfield Smoke Shop
20 Cedar Swamp Rd.
Smithfield
(401) 231-3909

By the Bay Smoke Shop
1680 Warwick Ave.
Warwick
(401) 921-5335

Humidor Smoke Shop
1732 Post Rd.
Warwick
(401) 732-3311

Mecca Lounge, The
650 Greenwich Ave.
Warwick
(401) 921-3668

3 Guys Cigar Co.
2077 W. Shore Rd.
Warwick
(401) 732-0878

Wonderland Smoke Shop
666 East Ave.
Warwick
(401) 823-3134

Mr J's Havana Shop
90 W. Warwick Ave.
West Warwick
(401) 822-0536

SOUTH CAROLINA
Marcella's Fine Cigars-Tobacco
161 S. Aiken Lane
Aiken
(803) 649-0377

Piedmont Tobacco Co.
3300 N. Main St., Ste. K
Anderson
(864) 224-4004

Taylors Tobacco
105 S. Main St.
Bishopville
(803) 484-4274

Peaceful Henry Inc.
181 Bluffton Rd.
Bluffton
(843) 757-0557

Tobacco Corner
510 E. Dekalb St.
Camden
(803) 432-4735

Coastal Cigars
4 Carriage Lane
Charleston
(843) 225-5233

Island Tobacco
808 Folly Rd.
Charleston
(843) 225-5202

Kingston Cigar Shop
1890 Sam Rittenberg Blvd.
Charleston
(843) 573-9911

Lianos Dos Palmas Handmade
   Cigars
52½ Wentworth St.
Charleston
(843) 723-4848

Lowcountry Tobacco
2578 Ashley River Rd.
Charleston
(843) 573-0601

Smoker Friendly
630 Skylark Dr.
Charleston
(843) 402-0130

Smoking Lamp
401 King St.
Charleston
(843) 577-7339

Tinder Box
177 Meeting St.
Charleston
(843) 853-3720

Tobacco Spot
2280 Savannah Hwy.
Charleston
(843) 571-2600

Tobacco Market
232 2nd St.
Cheraw
(843) 537-6390

Dsposable Cigar Tubes
141 Pelham Dr. 248
Columbia
(864) 513-1584

Lite Um Up Cigars Lounge
4435 Hard Scrabble Rd.
Columbia
(803) 708-4877

Modern Age Tobacco & Gifts
Colonial Village Shopping
   Center
1410 Colonial Life Blvd. #200
Columbia
(804) 772-2217

The Cigar Box
2910 Rosewood Dr.
Columbia
(803) 988-1423

Tobacco Merchant
1220 Bower Pkwy.
Columbia
(803) 749-5499

Tobacco Merchant
10136 Two Notch Rd.
Columbia
(803) 419-7428

Tobacco Market
2270 Hwy. 544
Conway
(843) 347-7099

Tobacco Corner
2109 E. Main St.
Duncan
(864) 433-0062

Tobacco Market
2191 W. Evans St.
Florence
(843) 667-9775

Tobacco Market
1593 S. Irby St.
Florence
(843) 665-7999

Smoker Shop & Cigars
2000 Hwy. 160, Ste. 103
Fort Mill
(803) 548-9531

Humidor
725 Front St.
Georgetown
(843) 546-1907

Halfway to Habana
631 S. Main St.
Greenville
(864) 232-9224

Illusions Smoke Shop
1041 W. Blue Ridge Dr.
Greenville
(864) 370-9090

Leaf-N-Match Ltd.
233 N. Main St.
Greenville
(864) 271-9080

Outland Gift & Cigar
700 Haywood Rd.
Greenville
(864) 297-4350

Outman Knife & Cigars
26 Orchard Park Dr.
Greenville
(864) 297-4350

Smokin Aces
701A W. Parker Rd.
Greenville
(864) 236-5935

Smokin Joes Tobacco & Gifts
2700 Poinsett Hwy.
Greenville
(864) 271-3932

Tobacco Unlimited
1624 Woodruff Rd.
Greenville
(864) 288-8805

Up In Smoke
1005 N. Pleasantburg Dr.
Greenville
(864) 233-1568

Tobacco Plus
1921 Hwy. 101 S.
Greer
(864) 968-1133

Tobacco Market
333 S. 5th St.
Hartsville
(843) 383-8812

Island Cigars
1000 William Hilton Pkwy.
Hilton Head Island
(843) 785-6633

Carolina Cigars
45 Pembroke Dr., #155
Hilton Head Isle
(843) 681-8600

Smoke Stack Ltd., The
33 Office Park Rd., #222
Hilton Head Isle
(843) 785-5599

Tobacco Road
119 Arrow Rd., #B
Hilton Head Isle
(843) 341-6265

Maduro Room
5175 Sunset Blvd.
Lexington
(803) 957-3547

Rossi Peter
401 Plantation Dr.
Lexington
(803) 957-5276

Low Country Pipe & Cigar
2 Hwy. 90 E.
Little River
(843) 281-9361

Vices Smoke Shop
1479 US 17
Little River
(843) 249-8492

Tobacco Shop
302 N.W. Front St.
Mullins
(843) 464-7996

Low Country Cigar House
3335 Business Hwy. 17 S.
Murrells Inlet
(843) 652-4427

East End Cigar Co.
7710 N. Kings Hwy.
Myrtle Beach
(843) 839-4499

Kilgor Trouts
512 8th Ave. N.
Myrtle Beach
(843) 445-2800

Nick's Cigar World
1400 29th Ave. N.
Myrtle Beach
(843) 839-8266

Purple Haze Smoke Shop
4504 Socastee Blvd.
Myrtle Beach
(843) 293-3420

Tinder Box
1301 Celebrity Circle
Myrtle Beach
(843) 444-5690

Nick's Cigar World
2705 Hwy. 17 S.
North Myrtle Beach
(843) 361-8266

J A Cigars
2910 Hwy. 86
Piedmont
(864) 307-9437

Bullseye Cigar Cutters
209 Archie Ware Rd.
Ridge Spring
(803) 649-4592

Tobacco Hut
1016 N.E. Main St.
Simpsonville
(864) 962-8622

C. Edward Cigars
113 N. Church St.
Spartanburg
(864) 573-7811

Sir Tom's Tobacco Emporium
2811 Reidville Rd.
Spartanburg
(864) 587-1566

Kingston Cigar Shop
1525 Old Trolley Rd.
Summerville
(843) 832-4446

Lighthouse Cigars & Gifts
717 Central Ave.
Summerville
(843) 261-2442

Sir Williams Tobacco
1064 Broad St.
Sumter
(803) 774-8484

Tobacco Market
5680 Broad St.
Sumter
(803) 494-3591

Surfside Tobacco
1702 Hwy. 17
Surfside Beach
(843) 233-8200

Big J's Tobacco
3234 Wade Hampton Blvd.
Taylors
(864) 244-5400

Tobacco Shop
1603 Hampton St.
Walterboro
(843) 549-9788

Smokers Depot
821 E. Liberty St.
York
(803) 628-1088

SOUTH DAKOTA
Deadwood Tobacco Co. &
   Cigar Bar
628 Lower Main St.
Deadwood
(605) 722-1510

Yst Smoke Shop
38574 State Hwy. 46
Lake Andes
(605) 487-7667

Kongo Office
4901 N. Main St.
Mitchell
(605) 996-0031

Discount Smoke Shop
718 Saint Patrick St.
Rapid City
(605) 336-3285

InLife For Life
2785 Ardee Ave.
Rapid City
(605) 390-0985

Stogies Smoke Shop
3064 Covington St.
Rapid City
(605) 716-3834

Tinder Box
520 7th St.
Rapid City
(605) 341-8466

Vino100/TinderBox
520 7th St.
Rapid City
(605) 341-8466

Smoke Shop
924 W. 3rd St.
Redfield
(605) 472-2519

Eastwold Smoke Shop
136 S. Phillips Ave.
Sioux Falls
(605) 332-2071

Fogies Stogies
5020 S. Marion Rd.
Sioux Falls
(605) 274-2400

J J's Wine Spirits & Cigars
4810 S. Western Ave.
Sioux Falls
(605) 357-9597

Dakota Tobacco Co.
1 9th Ave. S.E.
Watertown
(605) 886-5587

Midtown Smoke Shop & Casino
1 1st Ave. N.E.
Watertown
(605) 886-2204

Tobacco Road
901 Broadway St.
Yankton
(605) 665-7057

TENNESSEE
Tobacco Place
109 N. Main St.
Bolivar
(731) 658-9560

Olde World Leaf & Ale
101 Creekside Xing, Ste. 900
Brentwood
(615) 373-6815

Stogie's Ales and Fine Cigars
1800 Carothers Pkwy.
Brentwood/Cool Springs
(615) 377-7727

Bell's Smoke Shop
2700 Broad St.
Chattanooga
(423) 267-0785

Bell's Smoke Shop
3948 Brainerd Rd.
Chattanooga
(423) 624-9510

Bell's Smoke Shop
115 Browns Ferry Rd.
Chattanooga
(423) 825-1110

Burns Tobacconist
110 Jordan Dr.
Chattanooga
(423) 855-5200

Burns Tobacconist
725 Cherry St.
Chattanooga
(423) 267-7740

Sims Tobacco
3220 Wilcox Blvd.
Chattanooga
(423) 702-5321

Briar & Bean of Ciku
105 Fairview Lane
Clarksville
(931) 552-6465

Southern Light Farm
3453 Rossview Rd.
Clarksville
(931) 358-2520

Mo Thangz
3213 Hwy. 70 N.
Crossville
(931) 456-6181

Bell's Smoke Shop
260 16th Ave.
Dayton
(423) 570-9945

Bears Den Cigar Shop
108 W. College St.
Dickson
(615) 446-4455

Old Havana Smoke Shop
103 International Dr.
Franklin
(615) 771-6767

Woody's Smokes & Brews
1935 Mallory Lane
Franklin
(615) 778-9760

G & B Tobacco—The
  Gatlinburlier
611 Pkwy.
Gatlinburg
(865) 436-9177

Smokezy Tobacco & Pipes
431 Pkwy.
Gatlinburg
(865) 430-7779

Smokies Market & Tobacco
952 Pkwy.
Gatlinburg
(865) 436-5308

Cigar Depot
3040 Forest Hill Irene Rd. 102
Germantown
(901) 755-7279

Ye Olde Pipe Shoppe
581 Old Hickory Blvd.
Jackson
(731) 668-8999

Cigars and More
7600 Kingston Pike
Knoxville
(865) 470-0090

Excelsior Inc.
118 S. Central St.
Knoxville
(865) 546-6872

Leaf & Ale
9290 Kingston Pike S.W.
Knoxville
(865) 690-4772

Off the Wall
8805 Kingston Pike S.W.
Knoxville
(865) 693-3722

Silo Cigars
10947 Kingston Pike
Knoxville
(865) 675-7456

Smoke Pit
7316 Norris Freeway
Knoxville
(865) 922-0951

Smokin Joes
6110 Papermill Dr.
Knoxville
(865) 584-9010

Whatever
1823 Cumberland Ave.
Knoxville
(865) 544-7555

Jimmy's Tobacco Store
400 Old Nashville Hwy.
LaVergne
(615) 793-4810

Cigar Club
2148 N. Gallatin Rd.
Madison
(615) 859-2425

Memphis Tobacco Bowl
152 Madison Ave.
Memphis
(901) 525-2310

Smokers Shop
2564 Appling Rd.
Memphis
(901) 213-0616

Tinder Box, The
2760 N. Germantown Pkwy.
Memphis
(901) 381-2775

Tobacco Corner Ltd.
669 S. Mendenhall Rd.
Memphis
(901) 682-3326

Tobacco King
2204 Whitten Rd.
Memphis
(901) 387-1224

United Smoke Shop
2618 Frayser Blvd.
Memphis
(901) 353-0420

Whatever
610 S. Highland St.
Memphis
(901) 452-4731

Wizard's
1999 Madison Ave.
Memphis
(901) 726-6800

Tobacco Junction Inc.
7863 US Hwy. 51 N.
Millington
(901) 873-2800

City Smoke Shop LLC
1205 Shields Ferry Rd.
Morristown
(423) 587-2262

Liquid Smoke
2 Public Square
Murfreesboro
(615) 217-7822

Three Ten Pipe & Tobacco Shop
109 E. Main St.
Murfreesboro
(615) 893-3100

Arcade Smoke Shop
11 Arcade
Nashville
(615) 726-8031

Belle Meade Premium Cigars
  and Gifts
4518 Harding Pike
Nashville
(615) 297-7963

Elliston Place Pipe & Tobacco
2204 Elliston Place
Nashville
(615) 320-7624

Havana Smoke Shop
433 Opry Mills Dr.
Nashville
(615) 514-2826

Marivuana Hempsalots
   Store & Café
1810 Shelby Ave.
Nashville
(615) 228-4444

Smoke & Ale
519 Donelson Pike
Nashville
(615) 889-1821

Smoke Depot of Nashville Inc.
563 Stewarts Ferry Pike
Nashville
(615) 391-4171

Tobacco Road Coffee & Smoke
   Shop
15551 Old Hickory Blvd.
Nashville
(615) 331-7139

Uptown's Smoke Shop
4001 Hillsboro Rd.
Nashville
(615) 292-6866

Southside Tobacco Shop
2061 Hwy. 641 S.
Parsons
(731) 847-6632

Bad Habits
208 E. Grigsby St.
Pulaski
(931) 363-0545

Bell's Smoke Shop
222 Sequoyah Rd.
Soddy Daisy
(423) 332-0626

Bell's Smoke Shop
690 Hwy. 72
South Pittsburg
(423) 837-2967

TEXAS

Jerry's
1465 Pine St.
Abilene
(325) 673-8333

Leaf, The
202 Cypress St.
Abilene
(325) 670-9955

Smokin Jo's Discount Tobacco
2757 S. 1st St.
Abilene
(325) 677-2006

Addison Cigar & Tobacco
15401 Addison Rd.
Addison
(972) 239-1521

Cigar Shop & More
4285 Belt Line Rd.
Addison
(972) 661-9136

Jones-Cowan Pipe & Tobacco
2497 I-40, Frontage Rd.
Amarillo
(806) 355-2821

Smoke Shop
2413 Hobbs Rd.
Amarillo
(806) 353-6331

Arlington Cigar
827 N.E. Green Oaks Blvd.
Arlington
(817) 226-7441

Pipedream
1308 S. Cooper St.
Arlington
(817) 261-0218

Smoke City 2
4720 W. Sublett Rd.
Arlington
(817) 483-8139

Smokey's House of Pipes
2700 E. Randol Mill Rd.
Arlington
(817) 649-8720

Tobacco Lane
3811 S. Cooper St.
Arlington
(817) 784-0022

Tobacco Roads & Gifts
3118 S. Cooper St.
Arlington
(817) 467-7623

BC Smoke Shop Austin
2001 Guadalupe St.
Austin
(512) 474-0420

Bobalu Cigar Co.
509 E. 6th St.
Austin
(512) 469-5877

Cigar Palace
817 Congress Ave.
Austin
(512) 472-2277

Gas Pipe
701 E. 5th St.
Austin
(512) 472-4774

Habana House
3601 S. Congress Ave., #D
Austin
(512) 447-9449

Heroes & Legacies
10000 Research Blvd.
Austin
(512) 343-6600

Oat Willie's
617 W. 29th St.
Austin
(512) 482-0630

Oat Willie's South
1931 E. Oltorf St.
Austin
(512) 448-3313

Planet K Texas
11657 Research Blvd.
Austin
(512) 502-9323

Planet K Texas
1516 S. Lamar Blvd.
Austin
(512) 443-2292

Tobacco Station USA
6225 N. Lamar Blvd.
Austin
(512) 454-9110

Tobaccoville Inc.
5330 Manchaca Rd.
Austin
(512) 851-1741

Cigar Shoppe
2113 Harwood Rd.
Bedford
(817) 545-5141

Dragons Breath
2301 Central Dr.
Bedford
(817) 355-8877

3R's Cigars
949 N. Hwy. 67
Cedar Hill
(972) 293-3777

Tobacco Cabana
265 Hickerson St.
Cedar Hill
(469) 272-5999

City Cigars
3001 Knox St.
Dallas
(214) 528-5700

Dallas Cigar
6162 Greenville Ave.
Dallas
(214) 373-9993

E Z Way Smoke Shop
  Accessories
11029 Harry Hines Blvd.
Dallas
(972) 331-5706

Sir Elliot's Tobacco & Coffee
18101 Preston Rd.
Dallas
(972) 250-4630

3R's Cigars
100 S. Main St. 116
Duncanville
(972) 572-4427

Town & Country Cigars
1301 W. Glade Rd.
Euless
(817) 358-8862

Bon Ton Roule Fine Cigars
6500 Camp Bowie Blvd.
Fort Worth
(817) 763-0002

Funky Town Smoke Shop
3204 Camp Bowie Blvd.
Fort Worth
(817) 348-0084

Fusion Inc.
2205 W. Berry St.
Fort Worth
(817) 921-5500

Habits Smoke Shop
6625 N. Beach St.
Fort Worth
(817) 847-6332

Pop's Safari
2929 Morton St.
Fort Worth
(817) 334-0563

Smokies House of Pipes
6031 Camp Bowie Blvd.
Fort Worth
(817) 377-0149

Tobacco Lane on the Square
512 Main St.
Fort Worth
(817) 334-0900

Tejas Smoke Depot
1639 US 290
Fredericksburg
(830) 990-1472

Cigar Shop & More
5435 N. Garland Ave.
Garland
(214) 703-9399

Grapevine Cigar Tobacco
120 S. Main St.
Grapevine
(817) 424-2326

B C Smoke Shop
10950 FM 1960 Rd. W.
Houston
(281) 897-0420

Bomb Smoke Shop
1015 Nasa Rd. 1
Houston
(281) 282-2055

Briar Shoppe
2412 Times Blvd.
Houston
(713) 529-6347

Downing Street Ltd.
2549 Kirby Dr.
Houston
(713) 523-2291

Lone Star Tobacco
3741 FM 1960 W.
Houston
(281) 444-2464

Santa Barbara Cigars
11693 Westheimer Rd. 180
Houston
(281) 293-0609

Serious Cigars
6608 FM 1960 Rd. W.
Houston
(281) 397-9800

Smoke Dreamz
6447 Richmond Ave.
Houston
(713) 266-5554

Smoke Toys
4478 Hwy. 6 N., #B
Houston
(281) 345-8070

Texas Hookah
8403 Almeda Rd.
Houston
(877) 946-6524

Westbury Square Cigar Shop
5425 W. Bellfort St.
Houston
(713) 723-7200

Tobacco Lane
1101 Melbourne Rd.
Hurst
(817) 284-7251

Up In Smoke
7707 N. MacArthur Blvd.
Irving
(972) 556-0115

Easy's Tobacco
Golden Triangle Circle
Keller
(817) 379-0620

Cigar Box
2501 S. W S Young Dr.
Killeen
(254) 526-6811

Up in Smoke
2403 S. Stemmons Freeway
Lewisville
(972) 315-1300

Nothin' Butt Smokes
2267 34th St.
Lubbock
(806) 765-9355

Nothin' Butt Smokes
2812 4th St.
Lubbock
(806) 762-6613

Nothin' Butt Smokes
2502 79th St.
Lubbock
(806) 748-6785

Nothin' Butt Smokes
1730 Pkwy. Dr.
Lubbock
(806) 765-8905

Smoker's Haven
5102 60th St.
Lubbock
(806) 799-2489

Cigar Lounge
6840 Virginia Pkwy.
McKinney
(972) 540-5807

Cigars & More
2811 Craig Dr.
McKinney
(469) 952-5001

Hemingway
2200 W. Wadley Ave.
Midland
(432) 570-5333

Tobacco Haus Cigar Lounge
651 N. Business IH 35,
    Ste. 525
New Braunfels
(830) 620-7473

Filters Smoke Shop LLC
8401 Blvd. 26
North Richland Hills
(817) 581-2233

Town & Country Cigars
8200 N.E. Pkwy.
North Richland Hills
(817) 427-1777

Cigar Warehouse
2108 Dallas Pkwy.
Plano
(972) 608-5300

Sir Elliot's Tobacco
8608 Preston Rd.
Plano
(972) 681-4959

Two Brothers Cigars
1100 14th St.
Plano
(972) 424-7272

Stafford & Jones Tobacconist
2000 N. Plano Rd., Ste. 115
Richardson
(972) 907-8282

En Fuego
Summer Lee Dr.
Rockwall
(972) 771-4888

Tobacco Box Inc.
2787 Ridge Rd.
Rockwall
(972) 771-8800

C.I.G.A.R.
2235 Thousand Oaks Dr. 104
San Antonio
(210) 404-2626

Club Humidor
11745 W. IH 10, Ste. 140
San Antonio
(210) 558-7700

Club Humidor
204 Alamo Plaza
San Antonio
(210) 472-2875

Finck Cigar Co.
414 Vera Cruz
San Antonio
(210) 226-4191

Lazy Daze
3333 W. Ave.
San Antonio
(210) 541-0420

Planet K Texas—Evers
5619 Evers Rd.
San Antonio
(210) 521-5213

Gatsby, The
18730 Stone Oak Pkwy. 108
San Antonio
(210) 490-9340

Seguin Cigar
2021 W. Kingsbury St.
Seguin
(830) 303-7473

Dragon's Breath
1316 S. Vine Ave.
Tyler
(903) 593-0178

S & S Smoke Shop
3223 Wilbarger St.
Vernon
(940) 552-2228

Don's Humidor & Coffee Beans
1412 N. Valley Mills Dr.
Waco
(254) 772-3919

Smoke Ring
17050 Hwy. 3
Webster
(281) 332-9871

UTAH
Stogies
101 N.W. State Rd.
American Fork
(801) 763-7561

Gabbys Smoke Shop Cultural
5337 W. 1275 S.
Cedar City
(435) 867-5113

Deja Vu Smoke Shop
1917 W. 1800 N.
Clearfield
(801) 773-3525

Smoke & More
310 State St.
Clearfield
(801) 825-4830

Layton Smoke Shop
715 N. Main St.
Layton
(801) 889-0822

Earthly Awakenings
21 Federal Ave.
Logan
(435) 755-8657

Timberline Smoke Shop
1496 N. Main St.
Logan
(435) 787-1727

Smokin' Joe's Inc.
148 W. Center St.
Midvale
(801) 256-3318

Smokees Tobacco
509 W. Main St.
Mt. Pleasant
(435) 462-5472

Free Smoke
6191 S. State St.
Murray
(801) 281-6683

Smokes 4 U
657 W. 5300 S.
Murray
(801) 313-0202

One Stop Smoke Shop
2062 Harrison Blvd.
Ogden
(801) 393-2551

Smoker Friendly
333 2nd St.
Ogden
(801) 392-1258

Smoker's Choice
305 36th St.
Ogden
(801) 627-1727

Store
455 24th St.
Ogden
(801) 621-8854

This That & the Other
2620 S. Washington Blvd.
Ogden
(801) 621-4076

Whatever Etc.
2620 S. Washington Blvd.
Ogden
(801) 334-8776

Stogies
410 S. Freedom Blvd.
Provo
(801) 373-4019

Puff N Stuff
5434 S. 1900 W.
Roy
(801) 776-6004

Smoker's Delite
3570 W. 5600 S.
Roy
(801) 985-1048

Aztec Hwy. LLC
89 W. 3300 S.
Salt Lake City
(801) 466-2235

City Smoke Shop
2987 W. 3500 S.
Salt Lake City
(801) 955-6667

Ed's Smoke Shop
3157 W. 5400 S.
Salt Lake City
(801) 955-4707

Guru House of Hookah Smoke
   Shop
4523 S. Redwood Rd.
Salt Lake City
(801) 268-4041

J M Smoke Shop
2584 W. 4700 S.
Salt Lake City
(801) 969-3914

Jeanie's Smoke Shop
156 S. State St.
Salt Lake City
(801) 322-2817

Knuckleheads
443 E. 400 S.
Salt Lake City
(801) 533-0199

Loca Tienda Smoke Shop
5633 W. 6200 S.
Salt Lake City
(801) 955-6064

One Stop Smoke Shop
4645 S. 4000 W.
Salt Lake City
(801) 840-0689

One Stop Smoke Shop
1427 S. 300 W.
Salt Lake City
(801) 467-2933

Pharoah's Smoke Shop
3925 S. State St.
Salt Lake City
(801) 266-1711

Salt City Cigars
1877 Fort Union Blvd.
Salt Lake City
(801) 943-3481

Shop Smoke & Drink
3197 S. Redwood Rd.
Salt Lake City
(801) 886-0116

Smoke Shop
791 E. 3300 S.
Salt Lake City
(801) 484-0456

Smoker Friendly
824 W. N. Temple
Salt Lake City
(801) 531-7995

Smokers Connection
1661 W. 4100 S.
Salt Lake City
(801) 281-5949

Smokers Guru Smoke Shop
and Hooka
1350 S. State St.
Salt Lake City
(801) 953-1350

Tinder Box
188 E. Winchester St.
Salt Lake City
(801) 268-1321

Tobacco Max
3149 S. State St.
Salt Lake City
(801) 487-2197

Tobacco Max
1568 S. State St.
Salt Lake City
(801) 466-4206

Tobacco Store
320 E. 3900 S.
Salt Lake City
(801) 743-6360

Up in Smoke
3601 Constitution Blvd.
Salt Lake City
(801) 963-5700

Wizards & Dreams
1169 S. State St.
Salt Lake City
(801) 486-2505

Hungry Trout Cigars and
Smoke Shop
8634 S. 700 E.
Sandy
(801) 566-5178

VIP Smokes & Hookah
10330 S. Redwood Rd.
South Jordan
(801) 878-7851

Stogies
84 N. 100 W.
Spanish Fork
(801) 798-0092

Earrings & More Tattoos 4 U
Smoke Shop
695 N. Bluff St.
St. George
(435) 674-2431

Mike's Smoke & Cigar Gifts
1973 W. Sunset Blvd.
St. George
(435) 986-2028

Gabby's Smoke Shop—Cultural
Imports & Gifts
520 W. Telegraph St., Ste. 3
Washington
(435) 627-1494

Smoke Shop 101
6271 Dixie Dr.
West Jordan
(801) 963-3733

Smoke Zone & Gift
7093 Redwood Rd.
West Jordan
(801) 568-0583

VERMONT
Fired-Up
379 S. Barre Rd.
Barre
(802) 479-0438

A Kind Place
106 North St.
Bennington
(802) 442-2220

Hidden Treasures Smokin'
Shop
200 Lower Main
Johnson
(802) 635-9420

Pipestudio
4692 Main
Manchester
(802) 362-5589

Pipeworks and Wilke
420 E. Main St.
Middlebury
(802) 223-6110

Howie's Humidor
1174 Williston Rd., Ste. 5
South Burlington
(802) 864-7840

Emporium Tobacco and Gift
Shop
5 Green St.
Vergennes
(802) 877-6897

VIRGINIA
Best Smokes
8702 Richmond Hwy.
Alexandria
(703) 619-2780

Cigar Vault
6242C Little River Turnpike
Alexandria
(703) 750-9532

John Crouch Tobacco
215 King St.
Alexandria
(703) 548-2900

Old Virginia Tobacco Co.
5860 Kingstowne Center
Alexandria
(703) 971-1933

Duke Cigar & Tobacco
7354 Little River Turnpike
Annandale
(703) 256-3475

Cigar Connection
1000 N. Randolph St.
Arlington
(703) 294-6363

Classic Cigars & British
Goodies
2907 Wilson Blvd.
Arlington
(703) 525-6510

Old Virginia Tobacco Co.
1100 S. Hayes St.
Arlington
(703) 415-5554

Blacksburg Pipe & Tobacco
408 N. Main St.
Blacksburg
(540) 951-8457

Smoker Friendly
529 Commerce Dr.
Bluefield
(276) 322-1431

Sidetrack Tobacco
523A State St.
Bristol
(276) 466-8450

Burke Cigar & Lounge
9558 Old Keene Mill Rd.
Burke
(703) 440-0678

Carrollton Tobacco Co.
23305 Sugar Hill Rd.
Carrollton
(757) 238-2056

Aficionados Smoke Shop
3447 Seminole Trail
Charlottesville
(434) 245-1175

Cavalier Pipe & Tobacco
1100 Emmet St. N.
Charlottesville
(434) 293-6643

C'Ville Smoke Shop
108 4th St. N.E.
Charlottesville
(434) 975-1175

Cigar Masters
1437 Sam's Dr.
Chesapeake
(757) 312-9889

John B Hayes Tobacconist
11755L Fair Oaks Mall
Fairfax
(703) 385-3033

Tobacco Express
18013 Forest Rd.
Forest
(434) 385-0639

Olde Towne Tobacconist
719 Caroline St.
Fredericksburg
(540) 371-3715

Tobacco Hut
5318 Plank Rd.
Fredericksburg
(540) 548-0088

Tobacco World
4183 Plank Rd.
Fredericksburg
(540) 785-1986

Leesburg Cigar & Pipe
205 Harrison St. S.E.
Leesburg
(703) 777-5557

Leesburg Emporium & Smoke
   Shop
205 Harrison St. S.E.
Leesburg
(703) 777-5557

Mister John's Tobacco Shop
817 Main St.
Lynchburg
(434) 847-3050

McLean Cigars PG Boutique
1429 Center St.
McLean
(703) 848-8095

Havana Connections Inc.
11645 Midlothian Turnpike
Midlothian
(804) 897-7307

Bond's Fine Cigar Shop
4165 William Styron Square
Newport News
(757) 223-9460

Lazy Dayz
731 J Clyde Morris Blvd.
Newport News
(757) 596-2907

Bond's Fine Cigar Shop
8111 Shore Dr.
Norfolk
(757) 502-7449

Emerson's of Norfolk
116 Granby St.
Norfolk
(757) 624-1520

Cigar Town Inc.
11903 Democracy Dr.
Reston
(703) 481-0055

A & K Tobacco Shop
3105 Mechanicsville Turnpike
Richmond
(804) 344-5443

Island Tobacco & Gifts
9125 W. Broad St.
Richmond
(804) 217-5604

Old Virginia Tobacco Co.
3532 W. Cary St.
Richmond
(804) 353-4675

Private Stock Cigar & Wine Co.
435 N. Ridge Rd.
Richmond
(804) 285-3760

Tobacco Store
11266 Patterson Ave.
Richmond
(804) 754-2280

Milan Tobacconists
309 S. Jefferson St.
Roanoke
(540) 344-5191

Tobacco Co.
5429 Williamson Rd.
Roanoke
(540) 366-6006

Top 21 Tobacco Plus
3201 Brambleton Ave.
Roanoke
(540) 725-1811

Select Leaf Tobacco Shop
325 Garrisonville Rd.
Stafford
(540) 720-2928

Churchill Cigars
1348 N. Great Neck Rd.
Virginia Beach
(757) 481-0346

Emerson's of Norfolk
4435 Virginia Beach Blvd.
Virginia Beach
(757) 493-9910

Old Dominion
5400 Virginia Beach Blvd.
Virginia Beach
(757) 497-1001

Papa Joes Smoke Shop
800 S. Lynnhaven Rd.
Virginia Beach
(757) 431-0061

Smoke Shack 1
1417 Lynnhaven Pkwy.
Virginia Beach
(757) 468-4011

Smoke Shack 5
1628 Independence Blvd.
Virginia Beach
(757) 309-4740

Valley Cigar Pub
405 W. Main St.
Waynesboro
(540) 943-5060

John B Hayes Tobacconist
50 E. Piccadilly St.
Winchester
(540) 545-7000

Octopus Garden
13626 Jefferson Davis Hwy.
Woodbridge
(703) 491-6118

Old Virginia Tobacco Co.
2745 Metro Plaza
Woodbridge
(703) 492-2260

Tobacco World 3
1948 Daniel Stuart Square
Woodbridge
(703) 497-6161

Tobacco Zone
14836 Build America Dr.
Woodbridge
(703) 494-1299

US 1 Tobacco
13448 Jefferson Davis Hwy.
Woodbridge
(703) 497-1984

Village Tobacco Yorktown
1900 George Washington Mem.
 Hwy., Ste. I
Yorktown
(757) 595-0405

WASHINGTON

Bellevue Cigar & Smoke Shop
1313 156th Ave. N.E.
Bellevue
(425) 643-9011

Fairhaven Smoke Shop
1200 Harris Ave.
Bellingham
(360) 647-2379

Smoke Time
17208 Bothell Way N.E.
Bothell
(425) 424-9099

Two Rivers Smoke Shop
5318 Chief Brown Lane
Darrington
(360) 436-2105

Des Moines Smoke Shop
21636 Marine View Dr. S.
Des Moines
(206) 870-3353

Everett Cigar & Tobacco
11108 Evergreen Way
Everett
(425) 348-3304

Everett Smoke Shop
5108 Evergreen Way 1
Everett
(425) 252-1900

B J's II Tobacco Co.
4315 Pacific Hwy. E.
Fife
(253) 922-6830

Indian Smoke Shop
1207 Alexander Ave. E.
Fife
(253) 922-7455

Cigar Land
6130 E. Lake Sammamish
 Pkwy. S.E., Ste. F
Issaquah
(425) 369-2496

Cigar Land
25451 104th Ave. S.E.
Kent
(253) 856-3199

Kent Smoke Shop
1601 W. Meeker St.
Kent
(253) 852-4356

Cigar City
12865 N.E. 85th St.
Kirkland
(425) 576-9599

Tobacco Patch
125 Central Way
Kirkland
(425) 739-4782

Indian Smoke Shop
7402 Pacific Hwy. E.
Milton
(253) 922-3001

J & J Smoke Shop
17 Crowder Rd.
Okanogan
(509) 422-4482

Fire & Earth
322 4th Ave. E.
Olympia
(360) 705-3976

Tobacco Depot #6
3995 Bethel Rd. S.E.
Port Orchard
(360) 895-2490

Cigar Land Puyallup
13414 Meridian E.
Puyallup
(253) 445-9989

Cigarland Canyon Rd.
11012 Canyon Rd. E.
Puyallup
(253) 531-8899

North Point Smoke Shop
6408 River Rd. E.
Puyallup
(253) 922-9345

Riverside Smoke Shop
7324 River Rd. E.
Puyallup
(253) 845-5622

Wholly Smoke
11904 Meridian E.
Puyallup
(253) 848-8008

World Cigar
15012 Meridian E, # 3
Puyallup
(253) 445-9950

Fine Wine & Cigars
16535 N.E. 76th St.
Redmond
(425) 869-0869

Smoke Time
15161 N.E. 24th St.
Redmond
(425) 641-8421

Valley Smoke & Cigars
17621 108th Ave. S.E.
Renton
(425) 255-5611

Cigar Land
714 228th Ave. N.E.
Sammamish
(425) 836-1667

A-Aall Shop
1501 Pike Place
Seattle
(206) 623-2698

Arcade Smoke Shop
1522 5th Ave.
Seattle
(206) 587-0159

Beenie's Smoke Shop
419 Cedar St.
Seattle
(206) 441-2746

Broadway Smoke Shop
219 Broadway E.
Seattle
(206) 324-6707

Dan's Smoke Shop
5901 24th Ave. N.W.
Seattle
(206) 297-6220

F. K. Kirsten Tobacconist
910 Lenora St.
Seattle
(206) 264-2966

Market Tobacco Patch
1906 Pike Place
Seattle
(206) 728-7291

Piece of Mind Fremont
315 N. 36th St.
Seattle
(206) 675-0637

Pikes Smoke Shop
1411 2nd Ave.
Seattle
(206) 223-0081

Rain City Cigar
5963 Corson Ave. S.
Seattle
(206) 767-2048

Sam's Smokes
4239 University Way N.E.
Seattle
(206) 547-5344

Still Smokin V
5261 University Way N.E.
Seattle
(206) 524-3769

University Smoke Shop
4519 University Way N.E.
Seattle
(206) 632-8891

C K Smoke Shop
457 W. Washington St.
Sequim
(360) 683-1919

Smoke Shop
2121 Olympic Hwy. N.
Shelton
(360) 426-0126

Young's Smoke Shop
16322 Pacific Ave. S.
Spanaway
(253) 539-3071

Tobacco World
621 W. Mallon Ave.
Spokane
(509) 326-4665

Piece of Mind
12101 E. 1st Ave.
Spokane Valley
(509) 922-9227

Greenroom, The
6413 6th Ave.
Tacoma
(253) 566-6436

Indian Smoke Shop II
5916 29th St. N.E.
Tacoma
(253) 568-8091

Lyle's 2 Smoke Shop's
3114 River Rd. E.
Tacoma
(253) 922-9041

Nate's Eastside Smoke Shop
4014 McKinley Ave.
Tacoma
(253) 473-2400

North Point Smoke Shop
6210 29th St. N.E.
Tacoma
(253) 952-7555

Tacoma Pipe & Tobacco
5602 S. Lawrence St.
Tacoma
(253) 475-7448

Thunderbird Aficionado Cigar
7121 Waller Rd. E.
Tacoma
(253) 531-8814

Tinder Box
7921 S. Hosmer St.
Tacoma
(253) 472-9993

Up in Smoke
8415 Steilacoom Blvd. S.W.
Tacoma
(253) 588-6009

Paul's Cigars
11600 S.E. Mill Plain Blvd.
Vancouver
(360) 885-3838

Cigar & Pipe
7 N. Wenatchee Ave.
Wenatchee
(509) 888-7380

Smoke City
212 5th St., #11B
Wenatchee
(509) 665-9001

All Star Cigar & Tobacco
14152 N.E. Woodinville
 Duvall Rd.
Woodinville
(425) 415-1301

Carrot's
609 Fruitvale Blvd.
Yakima
(509) 248-3529

Lil Brown Smoke Shack
3201 Goodman Rd.
Yakima
(800) 706-2480

WEST VIRGINIA
Dave's Emporium and Tobacco
 Shoppe
2964 Robert Centre Byrd Dr.
Beckley
(304) 252-3850

Smoker Friendly
19 Nell Jean Mall
Beckley
(304) 255-5510

NBS Smokehouse Inc.
103 S. Kanawha St.
Buckhannon
(304) 471-2045

Anchor Tobacco Company
605 Capitol St.
Charleston
(304) 342-6134

The Squire Tobacco Unlimited
108 Capitol St.
Charleston
(304) 345-0366

Smokers Choice LLC
120 Carolina Ave.
Chester
(304) 387-9800

Smoke Time Sam's
126 Milford St.
Clarksburg
(304) 622-2688

NBS Smokehouse Inc.
915 Country Club Rd.
Fairmont
(304) 368-1805

Tobacco Rd.
107 W. 2nd St.
Man
(304) 583-9320

Eclipse
513 W. King St.
Martinsburg
(304) 263-9982

NBS Smokehouse Inc.
740 Venture Dr.
Morgantown
(304) 292-8809

Slight Indulgence
407 High St.
Morgantown
(304) 292-3401

Westover Smokehouse
202 Holland Ave.
Morgantown
(304) 225-2530

Smoke Shak
401 6th St.
Point Pleasant
(304) 674-8104

Smokey's
4201 Freedom Way
Weirton
(304) 748-6900

WISCONSIN

Appleton Souvenir & Cigar Co.
415 W. College Ave.
Appleton
(920) 830-8349

Jerry's Tobacco & Book
322 W. College Ave.
Appleton
(920) 832-0527

Pages & Pipes
322 W. College Ave.
Appleton
(920) 734-2821

Pages & Pipes
748 W. Northland Ave.
Appleton
(920) 830-0309

Three Eagles Gift Shop
66096 Old US Hwy. 2
Ashland
(715) 682-8844

Jack's Tobacco & MCS
13640 W. Capitol Dr.
Brookfield
(262) 783-7473

Prime Cigar Co.
18900 W. Bluemound Rd.,
    Ste. 104
Brookfield
(262) 754-5220

Smokers Edge LLC
224 Litho St.
Coloma
(715) 228-3303

Charlie's Discount Tobacco
3604 E. College Ave.
Cudahy
(414) 768-9249

Lake Country Cigars
2566 Sun Valley Dr.
Delafield
(262) 646-7530

Smoke Shop LLC, The
127 Park Place
Delavan
(262) 740-7467

Briar & Bean
353 Main Ave.
DePere
(920) 336-6665

Hemmingway Cigar Bar
2960 Cahill Main
Fitchburg
(608) 270-3576

Smokes III
85 N. Pioneer Rd.
Fond Du Lac
(920) 907-0660

Metro Cigars LLC
W182N9606 Appleton Ave.,
    Ste. 104
Germantown
(262) 255-1996

Oneida Smoke Shops
2514 W. Mason St.
Green Bay
(920) 496-7872

Oneida Smoke Shops
2642 Packerland Dr.
Green Bay
(920) 405-1501

Oneida Smoke Shops
2020 Airport Dr.
Green Bay
(920) 592-8911

Tobacco World
4818 S. 76th St.
Greenfield
(414) 281-1935

S R Tobacco
5307 S. 108th St.
Hales Corners
(414) 427-0004

Pavilion
135 Main St.
Hayward
(715) 634-6035

St. Croix Cigar Co.
525 2nd St.
Hudson
(715) 386-4030

Flying High–Flag Store
421 N. Parker Dr.
Janesville
(608) 756-2280

Andrea's
2401 60th St.
Kenosha
(262) 657-7732

Briar Patch
519 Main St. N.E.
LaCrosse
(608) 784-8839

Smoke N Time
252 Center St.
Lake Geneva
(262) 248-7170

Cibao
640 W. Washington Ave.
Madison
(608) 256-1382

Knuckleheads Tobacco & Gifts
550 State St.
Madison
(608) 284-0151

Sunshine Daydream
434 State St.
Madison
(608) 250-2365

Tobacco Bar Ltd.
6613 Seybold Rd.
Madison
(608) 276-7668

Plaza Smoke Shop
N81W15092 Appleton Ave.
Menomonee Falls
(262) 250-9666

Famous Cigar
7030 W. North Ave.
Milwaukee
(414) 302-9904

Famous Smoke Shop
1213 E. Brady St.
Milwaukee
(414) 277-9904

Jones Smoke Shop & Grocery
4534 W. North Ave.
Milwaukee
(414) 875-9771

Knuckleheads
2949 N. Oakland Ave.
Milwaukee
(414) 962-3052

Smoker Choice
5021 W. Howard Ave.
Milwaukee
(414) 541-3291

Smoker's Club
10708 W. Oklahoma Ave.
Milwaukee
(414) 546-0525

Smoker's Club
4267 W. Layton Ave.
Milwaukee
(414) 325-7440

Smokers Haven
8064 N. 76th St.
Milwaukee
(414) 371-1732

Smokers Hub
1148 Miller Park Way
Milwaukee
(414) 645-8773

Tobacco One
801 E. Capitol Dr.
Milwaukee
(414) 964-6447

Uhle Tobacco Co.
114 W. Wisconsin Ave.
Milwaukee
(414) 273-6665

Tasting Room
6000 Monona Dr.
Monona
(608) 223-1641

Port Tobacco
215 N. Franklin St.
Port Washington
(262) 268-7801

Plaza Smoke Shop
3701 Durand Ave.
Racine
(262) 554-4777

Falls Smoke Shop
159 Concord Dr.
Sheboygan Falls
(920) 467-6311

Smokers Club
2410 10th Ave.
South Milwaukee
(414) 570-9911

Tobacco City
3046 E. Layton Ave.
St. Francis
(414) 486-9611

Tobacco Store
4698 S. Whitnall Ave.
St. Francis
(414) 744-2920

Stogy Stop
1307 Strongs Ave.
Stevens Point
(715) 345-7266

Elliott's on Jefferson Street
716 Jefferson St.
Sturgeon Bay
(920) 743-3172

Whitetail Crossing
27867 State Hwy. 21
Tomah
(608) 372-3721

Lorillard Tobacco Co.
N15W22180 Watertown Rd.,
   Ste. 9
Waukesha
(262) 524-9277

Nice Ash
327 W. Main St.
Waukesha
(262) 547-9009

Havanna Lounge & Cigar
9505 W. Greenfield Ave.
West Allis
(414) 258-8219

Smokes IV
2040 S. Main St.
West Bend
(262) 338-6662

WYOMING
E R Cigar and More
3702 Salt Creek Hwy.
Casper
(307) 577-5774

Rialto Cigar Store
100 E. 2nd St.
Casper
(307) 232-8662

Joey's Smoke Shop
416 Central Ave.
Cheyenne
(307) 634-3482

Smokes
1941 Sheridan Ave.
Cody
(307) 587-8493

Huff-N-Puff Smoke Shop
206 Yellowstone Hwy.
Douglas
(307) 358-1921

Tobacco Row
120 N. Cache St.
Jackson
(307) 733-4385

Junction Tobacco Shop
312 E. Grand Ave.
Laramie
(307) 742-2292

Up in Smoke
907 Shoshoni St.
Thermopolis
(307) 864-9434

CANADIAN CIGAR STORES

BRITISH COLUMBIA
Burning Desires Cigar Club
540 Beatty St.
Vancouver
(604) 681-6683

City Cigar
888 W. 6th Ave.
Vancouver
(604) 879-208

Shefield & Sons Tobacconist
712 Park Royal N.
West Vancouver
(604) 926-7011

Club Havana
15553 Marine Dr.
White Rock
(604) 542-0056

MANITOBA

River City Cigar Co. Ltd.
18th St.
Brandon
(204) 726-0472

United Cigar Stores
800 Rosser Ave,
Brandon
(204) 727-5284

Cindy's Smoke Shop
Fairford Indian Rsve.
(204) 659-5670

Arboc Smoke Shop and Gas
   Bar
4820 Portage Ave.
Headingley
(204) 831-1993

Core-Mark International Inc.
99 Bannister Rd.
Winnipeg
(204) 633-9244

Gateway News Stand
141-1225 Saint Mary's Rd.
Winnipeg
(204) 256-5432

La Mota
1859 Portage Ave.
Winnipeg
(204) 889-6566

Shefield & Sons.
1120 Grant Ave.
Winnipeg
(204) 452-3055

ONTARIO

The Walper Tobacco Shop
15 King St. W.
Kitchener
(519) 745-9984

Havana House
9 Davies Ave.
Toronto
(416) 406-6644

Smokin' Cigar, The
1699 Bayview Ave.
Toronto
(416) 545-0063

Thomas Hinds' Tobacconist
8 Cumberland St.
Toronto
(416) 757-0237

Yitz'z Humidor
346 Eglinton Ave. W.
Toronto
(416) 487-4506

Havana Tobacconist
2901 Bayview Ave.
Willowdale
(416) 733-9736

La Casa del Habano
473 Ouellette Ave.
Windsor
(519) 254-0017

QUEBEC

Blatter and Blatter Inc.
365 du President Kenne
Montreal
(514) 845-8028

Davidoff
1452 Rue Sherbrooke W.
Montreal
(514) 289-9118

Independent Cigar Store
506 Rue McGill
Montreal
(514) 844-4128

La Casa del Habano
1434 Sherbrooke Quest
Montreal
(514) 849-0037

Québec Cigare Inc.
55 Rue Du Sault-Au-Matelot
Quebec
(418) 265-6165

Rib N Reef Steakhouse
8105 Decarie Blvd.
Montreal
(514) 735-1601

Stogie's Cigar Lounge
2015 Crescent St.
Montreal
(514) 848-0069

Tabagie Stanley
1140 Boul De Maisonneuve
Montreal
(514) 843-4284

Tabagie de L'Hôtel Hilton
1100 Blvd. Rene-Levesque
   Est.
Quebec
(418) 522-5808

SASKATCHEWAN

RJ's Smoke Shop
110 Souris Ave.
Weyburn
(306) 842-4573

GLOSSARY OF TERMS

Aficionado or cigar aficionado: A person who is fond of smoking cigars; an expert on cigars and cigar smoking; a cigar enthusiast; a cigar lover.

Amarillo: A yellow wrapper leaf grown under shade.

Band or cigar band: A paper ring around the head of most cigars. Cigar bands are often printed with the name of the brand, country of origin, and/or indication that the cigar is hand-rolled. They often have colorful graphics, which have made them a popular collector's item.

Barrel: The main body of the cigar.

Belicoso: Traditionally a short, pyramid-shaped cigar, 5 or 5½ inches in length with a shorter, more rounded taper at the head and a ring gauge of 50 or less. Belicoso is often used to describe a corona or corona gorda with a tapered head.

Binder: The portion of leaf used to hold together the blend of filler leaves; with the wrapper and filler, it is one of the three main components in a cigar.

Blend: The mix of tobacco in a cigar, including up to five types of filler leaves, a binder leaf, and an outer wrapper.

Boite nature: The cedar box in which many cigars are sold.

Bouquet: The smell, or nose, of a fine cigar. A badly stored cigar can lose its bouquet.

Box: The container used to package cigars.

Box-pressed: The slightly square appearance taken on by cigars packed tightly in a box.

Bunch: Up to four different types of filler tobacco blended to create the body of the cigar. The bunch is held together by the binder.

Bundle: A packaging method designed with economy in mind that uses a cellophane overwrap. It usually contains twenty-five or fifty cigars, traditionally without bands. Bundles, oftentimes seconds of premium brands, are usually less expensive than boxed cigars.

Cabinet selection: Cigars packed in a wooden box rather than the standard cardboard or paper-covered cigar boxes. These are preferable when buying cigars for aging.

Candela: A bright green shade of wrapper, achieved by a heat-curing process that fixes the chlorophyll content of the wrapper while it's still in the barn. Also referred to as double claro.

Cap: A circular piece of wrapper leaf placed at the head of the cigar.

Capa: The cigar's wrapper (also called the binder).

Churchill: A large corona-format cigar.

Claro: The lightest in color (like milky coffee) wrapper, usually mild, also sometimes called a "natural."

Colorado: A medium-brown to brownish-red shade of wrapper tobacco. Colorado cigars are usually aromatic and are associated with well-matured cigars.

Corojos: Plants chosen to provide wrapper leaves and grown under a gauze sunscreen.

Corona: The most familiar size and shape for premium cigars: generally straight-sided with an open foot and a closed, rounded head.

Cubanito: Tobacco variety now grown in parts of Nicaragua, Honduras, and Mexico and said to be a direct descendant of the original Havana stock grown in Cuba.

Culebra: A cigar made of three panetelas braided together.

Curing: The process of drying newly harvested tobaccos.

Double claro: A cigar, greenish brown, from an unmatured leaf that was dried fast. These cigars are mild or bland with little oil. (See *Candela*.)

Double corona: A big cigar, generally 7½ to 8 inches by a 49 to 52 ring gauge. Also called prominente.

Draw: The flow of smoke from a cigar.

Entubar: A rolling method that originated in Cuba. Rather than booking the filler leaves, the roller folds each individual filler leaf back on itself, then bunches the leaves together. Proponents of this method say it creates superior air flow through the cigar, which results in a more even draw and burn.

Figurado: A Spanish term that refers to cigars of various shapes and sizes, such as belicosos, torpedos, pyramids, perfectos, and culebras.

Filler: The innermost layer of the cigar. The individual tobacco used in the body of the cigar. A fine cigar usually contains between two and five different types of filler leaves taken from different parts of the plant or sources. Handmade cigars have long fillers, whereas machine-made cigars usually contain smaller-cut leaf.

Finish: A tasting term referring to the taste that lingers on your palate after a puff. Mild cigars do not have much finish, either in terms of length or complexity, but stronger, more full-bodied cigars have distinctive flavors that linger.

Foot: The end of the cigar one lights. Most often it is pre-cut, except in the case of torpedos and perfectos.

Gran corona: A very large cigar; generally 9¼ inches by 47 ring gauge.

Guillotine cigar cutter: A type of cigar cutter preferred by many cigar smokers for its size and durability as well as the clean and even cut it makes on a cigar. It can be single-blade or double-blade, although the double-blade type is most common.

Gum: A vegetable adhesive used to secure the head of the wrapper leaf around the finished bunch.

Habana: A designation which, when inscribed on a cigar band, indicates that a cigar is Cuban. Not all Cuban cigars are marked with "Habana" or "Havana."

Handmade: A cigar made entirely by hand with high-quality wrapper and long filler. All premium cigars are handmade. Hand-rollers can generally use more delicate wrapper leaves than machines.

Hand-rolled: A cigar made entirely by hand with high-quality wrapper and long filler.

Head: The closed end of the cigar opposite from the end one lights.

Hot: Describes a cigar that is underfilled and has a quick, loose draw. Can cause harsh flavors.

Humidor: A room or a box, of varying size, designed to preserve or promote the proper storage and aging of cigars by maintaining a relative humidity level of 70 percent and a temperature of approximately 65 to 70°F.

Hygrometer: A device that indicates the humidity (percentage of moisture in the air); used to monitor humidor conditions.

Lance: A cutter used to pierce a small hole in the closed end of a cigar. Also called a piercer.

Lector: Traditionally, the person who reads to the cigar rollers while they work.

Ligero: One of the three basic types of filler tobacco. The name means light in Spanish, but this aromatic tobacco lends body to a blend.

Long filler: Filler tobacco that runs the length of the body of the cigar, rather than chopped pieces found in machine-made cigars.

Lonsdale: A long cigar; generally 6 to 6¾ inches by a 42 to 44 ring gauge, but there are many variations.

Machine-made: Cigars made entirely by machine, using heavier-weight wrappers and binders and, frequently, cut filler in place of long filler.

Maduro: A cigar, very dark brown in color.

Oil: The mark of a well-humidified cigar. Even well-aged cigars secrete oil at 70 to 72 percent relative humidity, the level at which they should be stored.

Oscuro: A cigar, black, very strong with little bouquet; not produced in large quantities.

Panetela: A long, thin cigar shape.

Parejos: Straight-sided cigars, such as coronas, panetelas, and lonsdales.

Perfecto: A distinctive cigar shape that is closed at both ends, with a rounded head; usually with a bulge in the middle.

Piercer: A cutter used to pierce a small hole in the closed end of a cigar. Also called a lance.

Plug: A blockage that sometimes occurs in the tobacco that can prevent a cigar from drawing properly.

Puro: A Spanish term used to distinguish a cigar from a cigarette. Modern usage refers to a cigar blended with tobaccos from a single country. (All Cuban cigars use 100 percent Cuban tobacco so all Cuban cigars are puros.) Also used to denote premium or high-quality cigars.

Pyramid: A sharply tapered cigar with a wide, open foot and a closed head.

Ring gauge: A measurement for the diameter of a cigar, based on 64ths of an inch. A 40 ring gauge cigar is 40/64ths of an inch thick. The fatter the cigar, the more developed and full its taste will be, and it is also said to burn cooler than thinner cigars.

Robusto: A substantial, but short cigar; traditionally 5 to 5½ inches by a 50 ring gauge.

Rosado: A Spanish term that means "rose-colored." It is used to describe the reddish tint of some Cuban-seed wrapper.

Seco: The Spanish word for dry, seco is a type of filler tobacco. It often contributes aroma and is usually medium-bodied.

Shade-grown: Wrapper leaves that have been grown under a tent. The filtered sunlight creates a thinner, more elastic leaf.

Short filler: Used mainly in machine-made cigars, it consists of chopped scraps of leaf. Short filler burns quicker and hotter than long filler.

Shoulder: The area of a cigar where the cap meets the body. If you cut into the shoulder, the cigar will begin to unravel.

Spanish cedar: The kind of wood that is used to make most cigar boxes and humidors.

Spill: A strip of cedar used to light a cigar when using a candle or a fluid lighter, both of which can alter the taste of the cigar.

Sun-grown: Tobacco grown in direct sunlight, which creates a thicker leaf with thicker veins.

Torcedor: A person who rolls cigars.

Torpedo: A cigar shape that features a closed foot, a pointed head, and a bulge in the middle.

Tubos: Cigars packed in individual wood, metal, or glass tubes to keep them fresh.

Tunneling: The unwelcome phenomenon of having your cigar burn unevenly. To prevent it, rotate your cigar now and then.

Vein: The rib of the tobacco leaf. A quality cigar should not be too heavily veined.

Vintage: When a vintage is used for a cigar, it usually refers to the year the tobacco was harvested, not the year the cigar was made.

Wedge cut: A V-shaped cut made in the closed end of a cigar.

Wrapper: The outermost layer of the cigar. Thin, high-grade leaves with elasticity are used to restrain the binder and filler of the cigar. Good wrappers usually have no visible veins. Colors vary due to the maturing process and may indicate strength of the cigar.

Memorable Smokes

Remembering a great cigar can be almost as fun as smoking one. The following pages are designed as a place to keep the labels of the truly memorable ones. We've left space where you can write in where you were, who you were with, what drink accompanied the smoke, and, most important, what you liked about the cigar. Take my word for this; when you go back a year or so later, you'll enjoy the memory and maybe be reminded that you need to buy that cigar again.

ABOUT THE AUTHOR

Never one to shy away from a fight, the author (who shall remain nameless—don't you look at the front cover!), spent more than twelve years in a convent where he honed his snark chops. Having been drummed out after the discovery he was Jewish (and a man), he joined the circus as a clown wrangler, stuffing as many as possible of those scary suckers into that little car.

But the literarry (sic) life called so he went into the publishing world, where he works (or doesn't) to this day. The author likes walks on the beach; staring longingly at old, outdated calendars; and eating uncooked hotdogs. He lives in an old plasma TV box on Highway 17 in Ithaca, New York.

Knock first.

Lawrence Dorfman, a discerning cigar smoker for thirty years, has been a publishing professional for almost as long, in between smokes. He is the author of *The Snark Handbook,* a weighty little tome on the art of verbal sparring. He favors Padrons, Fuentes, Camachos, and CAOs but will smoke anything good in a pinch. He lives in Hamden, Connecticut, and spends as much time as possible in the Owl Cigar Lounge in New Haven.

Connect with us on Facebook—The Cigar Lover's Compendium.

NEW HAVEN, CT

CIGAR LOUNGE & TOBACCONISTS SINCE 1934

The Owl Shop is a cigar aficionado's landmark in its own right. A New Haven institution located in the heart of Yale University, the Owl Shop was originally opened in 1934 by Joseph St. John and his wife, Catherine, who came to America from Greece in 1925. At what originally began as a bookstore, Joseph sold tobacco and mixed his own blends. After the death of her husband, Catherine kept the shop open and also retained two of the shop's original employees, one of whom is still with the shop today: Joe Lentine.

The Owl's storied history lives on through Joe Lentine, who began working at the Owl in 1960 and continues to blend pipe tobacco on-site today. The chronicle of the Owl Shop is the story of New Haven itself. During the heyday of the adjacent Shubert Theater, it was common to see the likes of Edward G. Robinson, Vincent Price, Van Johnson, Alec Guiness, Rex Harrison, Olivia de Havilland, or Helen Hayes visiting the shop.

In 1998, Glen Greenberg purchased the quaint tobacco shop and completely refurbished the space, creating an inviting, wood-and-leather interior replete with armchairs, couches, and custom-fitted cigar tables. "My intention was to create a warm atmosphere reminiscent of, and possibly an extension of, one's living room," says Greenberg. "The challenge was to do this without losing the inherent character and overall feeling of this classic tobacco shop." Greenberg has recently introduced a robust lineup of live music to the Owl. A jazz enthusiast, he has installed a sound stage in the rear of the cozy lounge, where he books live bands Monday through Wednesday. The resulting vibe is part speakeasy, part Blue Note, and completely unique.

Today, the Owl Shop still attracts a refreshingly mixed crowd of New Haven regulars, visiting dignitaries, and Yalies, while maintaining its fine reputation for being one of the best-quality tobacco shops and cigar lounges in the country. The Owl Shop offers a wide variety of Dominican and Nicaraguan cigars, a 400-square-foot walk-in humidor, full bar, tobaccos blended on-premises, and a full line of Owl Shop custom-made pipes.

THE OWL SHOP, 268 COLLEGE STREET, NEW HAVEN, CT 06510
www.owlshopcigars.com